"Richie Dear –
    In my book you're
"Tops" – Happy 50 and
many more.
            Love
                Essie

Mazel Tov!
You're Middle-aged

By the Same Author

My Rabbi Doesn't Make House Calls
So the Kids Are Revolting . . . ?

Mazel Tov! You're Middle-aged

by ALBERT VORSPAN

DOUBLEDAY & COMPANY, INC.

GARDEN CITY, NEW YORK   1974

ISBN: 0-385-00212-2
Library of Congress Catalog Card Number 73–83681

Contents

Preface

Some people (like me) grow old gracefully, while some (like you) have to be carried into their middle age kicking, thrashing and sucking wind. Socrates warned the aging not to stick together because every old-timer has a kvetch: "I cannot eat, I cannot drink; the pleasures of youth and love are fled away; there was a good time once, but now that is gone and life is no longer life."

But, look, Socrates had the smarts, but what did he really know? In writing this chutzpadik guide on how to hack our middle ages, I recall the words that a bright fourth-grade girl used to describe Socrates. She wrote: "Socrates was a Greek. He was quite a fellow. He went up and down the country telling people what to do. They poisoned him."

Nobody is perfect, so put away the hemlock and read the book already.

AV

1974

Mazel Tov!
You're Middle-aged

I

So Now You're Middle-aged

So you are now middle-aged. What did you expect, eternal youth? But what exactly is middle age? When does it start? When does it end? Must it go straight downhill? Later, we'll tell you how to hack it but, first, let's define what we're talking about.

Middle age has nothing to do with years. I don't care what anyone says; it's a *state of mind.* Some people, like your ten-year-old nephew, Arthur, are born middle-aged. Others, like Hubert Humphrey and Nelson Rockefeller, will be bouncy boys forever. Middle-aged people tend to think about the past a lot, send their children to get the newspaper from the lawn, spend three or four extra minutes on the potty and sing "There once was an Indian maid" in unguarded moments in the shower. The bane of middle age is the mirror, not the calendar.

The Encyclopedia Americana (which my wife bought twenty-five years ago when a young chap came to the door and persuaded her he was putting himself through college) defines middle age cryptically as "that period in which the feudal system was developed down to the events which led to its downfall."

But what does an encyclopedia know? Especially one nearing middle age itself. Young people believe that middle age starts at thirty and they won't trust anyone who has crossed that divide. Biologists assert that the middle-age period is between forty and sixty. But with the life span zooming ever upward, who is to say that middle age does not now begin at fifty? Dr. Yetta Fabbissiner, a distinguished former somaticist who has recently become slightly anti-somatic, has declared: "Middle age is not a biological fact. It is a state of mind. When you cease being horny 90 per cent of the time, you are middle-aged, even if you are only twenty-seven years of age. I have a ninety-two-year-old patient who is not yet middle-aged. Go figure."

Actually, middle age is your age plus ten. So why be so uptight?

Yet clearly we, the middle-aged, should be more conscious of ourselves. We are too complacent. We should revolt more. Why should we always be lost in the shuffle between youth and the senior citizens? The former get youth fare, the latter get medicare and we get zonked! The country is obsessed with youth and the senior citizens are now demanding increasing attention as well. But what about us in the middle? How about being fair to the mediocre and the middling also? After all, there are approximately thirty-one million of us Americans between the ages of fifty and sixty-four and that ain't hay!

We should begin to organize a potent middle-age movement—sitting in, lying in, praying in, ringing doorbells and watering the grass roots. Why not affirmative action for *us?* How about a quota of middle-aged in every college, football team and office? We should do this because justice demands that we receive better treatment, not merely because the statistics favor us. After all, statistics are tricky, let's face it. According to statistics, every human being has an average of one testicle, and that is manifestly wrong.

There is a saying in the Talmud that "a single coin in a bottle rattles, but a bottle full of coins makes no sound." Well, think of the bottle as America and it is the youth culture which rattles around like a single coin, making all the racket and ruckus. Think of the full bottle as quiet and substantial, representing the experience and wisdom of mature years. This may not help much, but it wouldn't hurt.

HOW TO KNOW YOU ARE IT

How do you know when you hit middle age? When you find yourself going to more funerals than graduations. When someone has to straighten you up, as if you were a human pretzel or an erector set, after a long automobile trip. When you cover the gray roots every four weeks instead of every four months. When you turn the newspaper to the obituary page and calculate the law of averages even before you look at the headlines or the sports. When your memory begins to get creaky and you read half as fast and remember half as much. When you need one pair of glasses for reading, another for driving and still another for finding the other glasses you lose daily. When you have to use saccharine instead of sugar in your coffee and then can't drink the coffee and still get to sleep. When you reach the point that when someone asks you how you feel, you tell him. When someone calls you up to tell you that something has happened, you anticipate calamity. When everything gives you a sense of déjà vu. When college kids begin to look like juveniles and policemen like boy scouts.

When you think that a lifetime guarantee was a better bargain twenty years ago. When you die a little every time a young parent asks your advice by starting: "When you were my age . . ." When you view a rainstorm on your golf day as nature conspiring against you personally. When you tell the same joke to the same people, without noticing their glazed eyes and suppressed smirks. When your neck begins to look like a chicken instead of a swan. When fatigue sets in after thirty minutes of playing with your grandchildren (ten minutes with anyone else's children). When you eat dinner in a superb Mexican restaurant, savoring every morsel of chimichanga, only to panic at the thought there's no Maalox in your closet and the drugstores are all closed!

If you see yourself in all or most of these vignettes, face it . . . you're getting up in the paint cards. *You* call it maturity, of course, but you may be well on your way to senility.

But, before we go any further, let's see how old you are and whether you qualify for this trip through the middle ages:

YOU CAN'T TELL IF YOU'RE REALLY MIDDLE-AGED
WITHOUT A SCORECARD

1. *Your wife's name is:*
   a. Althea
   b. Debra
   c. Shirley
   d. Heidi
   e. Dawn

2. *Little Orphan Annie was brought to you by the people who gave us:*
>   a. Yakima apples
>   b. Preparation H
>   c. Ovaltine
>   d. The Depression
>   e. The GIs

3. *H. V. Kaltenborn was:*
>   a. A rare blood disease
>   b. A German child with a cold
>   c. An American radio commentator
>   d. The first zeppelin
>   e. A Nazi defector

4. *Bronco Nagurski was:*
>   a. The wildest horse in the West
>   b. A Polish transvestite
>   c. An American football player
>   d. The cowboy in the Marlboro ads
>   e. A Watergate wireman

5. *Houdini was:*
>   a. An Italian spaghetti with clam sauce
>   b. Italian for "What's up?"
>   c. A Jewish magician
>   d. An Italian plumber in the White House
>   e. Arabic for "One for the road"

6. *Black Jack Pershing was:*
>   a. Best poker player in Altoona
>   b. A beautiful black horse
>   c. An American general
>   d. The first black madam in Philadelphia
>   e. Joe Louis' cut man

7. *Tammany was:*
>   a. A county in Ireland
>   b. Greek for "If you've got it, flaunt it"
>   c. New York's political gonifs

      d. Nixon's first political victim

      e. A tongue-tied auctioneer

8. *The $64,000 Question was:*

      a. Nixon's "Checkers" speech

      b. Who paid for the vicuna coat?

      c. A television show

      d. The Mickey Jelke case

      e. First asked by Charlie McCarthy

9. *Charlie Chan was:*

      a. The best Chinese restaurant in San Francisco

      b. First Chinese-American boxer

      c. Movie detective

      d. Mayor of Hoboken, New Jersey

      e. Chester Morris' original name

10. *Clint Hartung was:*

      a. Discoverer of acupuncture

      b. A small Havana cigar

      c. Baseball phenom

      d. Memo writer for ITT

      e. A Washington bagman

11. *Tom Mix's horse was named:*

      a. Phoenix

      b. Holy Roller

      c. Tony

      d. Crazy Legs Hirsch

      e. Silver

12. *Sewell Avery was:*

      a. The first astronaut

      b. Shot out of a cannon

      c. Carried out of Montgomery Ward

      d. First American to die in the Israeli War of Independence

      e. The first WASP to play for the Harlem Globetrotters

Scoring:

The correct answer in every case is *c*, as any fool can see. You get 5 points for every correct answer. If you scored less than 30, you are under twenty years of age. If you scored between 30 and 45, you are somewhere between twenty and thirty, but aging rapidly. If your score was between 45 and 50, you are thirty-nine years old. Any score over 50 spells middle age. A perfect score (60) means you are already, for all practical purposes, totaled, and you should wait quietly for the taxidermist to come and stuff you.

In any event, if you weren't smart enough to figure out that *c* is always correct, you are a low-grade moron regardless of age.

ACCEPT WITH A TOUCH OF KVETCH

So now we know what middle age is, and that we are truly into it. What do we do now? Accept it gracefully with only a touch of a kvetch. The kvetch is a primary tool in the survival kit of middle age. But exactly what is a kvetch? It is something like a whine, a wail, a sigh, a lament and a complaint all wrapped together in one sibilant combination. It knows neither race, religion, geography, age (indeed, the *young* are really the biggest kvetchers except that they call it *Protest*). The term derives, of course, from the specifically Jewish experience and it is redolent of centuries of anguish. But the kvetch is primordial and universal; Jews have no monopoly on it. Lately blacks have been kvetching even more than Jews; Italians are discovering its power; Russians, American Indians and Egyptians have proved themselves active kvetchers; and WASPs have more to kvetch about than anyone else.

How does one kvetch? How recognize a kvetch when one comes upon it? Simple. It drips with self-pity. It is wrung from the inner depths of angst. Even as a brief sigh, it has an eloquence that transcends language. It is spontaneous in that it cannot be exorcised by shrink or shaman. It is timeless—once a kvetch always a kvetch. And it is edged with self-mocking and ironic humor.

Classic example: Two men sit on a park bench. The first looks at the second and emits a profound, moving kvetch. The second heaves a pretty good kvetch of his own and they thus communicate heart to heart. Finally the first says: "Why don't you ask me what's wrong?" The second complies: "Okay, tell me, what's wrong?" Pause. "Don't ask," kvetches the first.

Kvetching is healthy and nourishing if, like alcohol and food, it is used in moderation. A kvetch used indiscriminately is self-defeating. The chronic kvetcher will be avoided like the village leper. No, husband the kvetch, even if you are the wife. Use it sparingly and judiciously. For example, the middle-aged kvetch should be reserved for the occasions of the *present*; it should generally not be thrown away on the future or the past.

Kvetching about the future is folly. In the first place, things never turn out as we imagine they will—they are either better or worse, so why waste your breath kvetching in advance? Secondly, the future is too inscrutable, so forget it. Could anyone have foreseen that it would be easier to get to the moon than to cross New York City? Or that if you dropped a match on the Cleveland waterfront you could set fire to Lake

Erie? Or that women, homosexuals and Chicanos would come storming out of the closets just when blacks and revolting youth stopped tearing up the pea patch? So, it is no good expending our middle-age kvetches upon the vagaries of an unpredictable future. Besides, actuarial tables being what they are, we don't have all that much future ahead of us to kvetch about. As my eighty-seven-year-old father said when the doctor told him he wasn't getting any younger, "I don't *want* to get *younger;* I want to get *older.*"

A CARDINAL RULE

It is equally pointless to kvetch about the PAST. What's done is done. If you start kvetching about the past, where do you stop? Will you go all the way back to Moses trying to get across the Red Sea while the silent majority of the Hebrews stood on the shore, kvetching that they couldn't swim, the dye in their robes would run in the cold water, and who is for going back to Egypt to get some curds and whey? No, a cardinal rule of growing up (or old) gracefully and creatively is *Don't kvetch about the past!* Don't even look back at the shambles of your previous life. Just as a person who fears heights should not look down, so *you* should never dwell on the path you've traversed. To kvetch about the past is to unleash a flood of opportunities missed, warning lights ignored, crossroads chosen wrongly, tracks badly covered, doors silently closing behind you. Santayana said that he who ignores history is doomed to repeat it. Just ignore Santayana. Lot's wife turned back to kvetch once too often and you can still see her now, a pillar of salt plunked down in the desolation of the Dead Sea. The past is prelude, and today is the first day of the rest of your life. Now *that* deserves a kvetch.

I have a friend who is always looking back and kvetching about the past. She is pushing fifty, but her head is full of relics of her past which still eat her heart out. "If only I had married Sam," she kvetches, conjuring up the memory of the shiny-faced sophomore who sat next to her in Murphy Hall at the University of Minnesota some thirty years ago. "We would be poor now; Sam was a nebbish, but we'd be happy and we would go to the baseball games and root for the Twins and eat peanuts and hold hands. Sam wasn't much to look at, but he was an orphan and at least we wouldn't have to go to those damned Family Circle meetings!"

What my friend does not remember is that Sam was also a chronic kleptomaniac, that he graduated from St. Cloud Reformatory instead of the U of M and that he is now the richest pornographer in Superior, Wisconsin. So what good does all this backward kvetching do her? Anyway, Sam didn't know she was alive even *then* and what she mistook as a dreamy and appealing glance was actually Sam casing her pocketbook. This shows you.

Backward kvetching has the added peril, adumbrated in the above example, that we falsify our past in any case. How many times have we listened to Cousin Harry describing his heroic war stories? Harry has developed an emotional investment in his own imaginings. He positively quivers when he re-enacts the sea battle at Iwo Jima. But do you know that the closest he ever got to action was a riot in Paul's Passion Pit in San Diego—and that on the day of the invasion of Iwo Jima, Seaman 2/c Harry was in Tacloban,

Philippines, "liberating" fifty quarts of fresh orange juice for the weird captain of his ship? We have to learn to face ourselves without masquerades or masks. To dwell on the past is, inevitably, to twist the material, to burnish it with imagination and to fashion a golem which will haunt the present and trespass upon the integrity of one's person.

Thomas Wolfe was not the only one to find that you can't go home again. In fact, it's even harder now in the television age than it was in Tom's day. Duncan Haskell grew up in Walla Walla, Washington, in the shadow of the prison which was the town's chief industry. What with the war, marriage and employment in the East, he didn't get back to Walla Walla for twenty years. Now a prosperous traveling salesman, Duncan decided one day (impulsively) to pick up a car in Seattle and visit the old homestead. Nostalgia had softened the contours of the town in Duncan's memory. Driving along in a miasma of childhood memories, he suddenly found himself in a sea of neon signs, hamburger stands and shopping centers. Traffic ground to a halt. Impatiently he yelled to the chap alongside, "How far to Walla Walla?" The guy stared. "This *is* Walla Walla!" Sure enough, there in the distance was the prison, now gaily decorated with Chagall murals and restyled as a pagoda by the Japanese architect Taka Metziah.

Duncan remembered that his dearest boyhood chum, Alvin Cooper, lived next to the prison. Why not just drop in and chew the fat with Alvin? Remarkably, Alvin answered the ring, looking none the worse for wear, bright as a button, relaxed in shorts, sandals and puffy jowls.

"Well, I'll be damned if it isn't old Duncan, the pride of the East."

"You old sonofabitch, Alvin, you haven't changed a bit."

"Duncan Haskell, the biggest shithead of Walla Walla!"

"Alvin, you old ass-bandit, tell me what the hell you're up to!"

So Duncan went in, they had a gin and tonic, reminisced about the pranks of their childhood, swore at each other a few more times, grinned significantly, smoked two cigars each, playfully punched each other's shoulders, and filled in the missing twenty years in five minutes of broad-brush strokes—and lapsed into silence.

"Hey," said Alvin, "Seattle is on the 'Game of the Day.' Okay?"

"Sure," said Duncan, "why not?" And so the childhood friends, adult strangers, submitted to the idiot box and when Duncan took his leave, with men on second and third in Seattle's half of the eighth inning, Alvin was too excited to notice his departure. . . .

A similar thing happened when Roger's tank was blown up during the Korean war. Slightly injured, Roger was given two days' home leave. He flew to Kennedy, got a cab to Lynbrook and burst in upon his parents who had been worried to death by the War Department's telegram of his injury. They embraced in tears. The parents sat him down and asked him to tell them all about it. Roger complied and got to the point of the saga where his tank came under enemy fire outside of Seoul.

"Oh, listen, Roger," said his father, jumping to his feet. "Can you hold it a minute. 'I Love Lucy' is on."

Roger never finished. He felt like the longest commercial in Lynbrook. So don't look back, and don't
kvetch about the past. It's kaput, so don't make trouble.

THERE IS A PLACE EVEN FOR YOU IN THIS REVOLUTION

The real questions lie in the NOW. They are: *Who*
am I? *What* am I? And *where* am I in the universe?
Those are the acute questions and you'd better find
the answers.

Life is like a record that can't be played over again.
So the question before you—and the one to which this
book is dedicated—is: What are you doing with the
flip side of your life?

You don't have to be pollyannish to believe that
you can do better on the flip side. You needn't swallow
the canards about life beginning at forty to find ways
to make your remaining years brighter and richer than
those you've already wasted. *It can be done.* And this
valuable little book, if used judiciously, can be your
travel guide to hacking the middle ages and beyond.
Someone has called satire the ritual slaughter of sacred
cows, and this book is a shechitah for growing old.

We are living in the midst of a revolution . . . not a
political or economic revolution despite the cries of the
hot-eyed, but a *cultural* revolution—a revolution of
values—and America, that much-maligned and trou-
bled object of calumny, is where this revolution is at.
What is happening in America is a desperate search
for meaning and purpose. Less affluent people in the
world must worry about making a living and, of course,
so must we. But our deepest concern has become how
to make a life, not just a living. This is the real signifi-
cance of the youth revolt, the ecology movement, the

women's lib uprising and the challenges to suburbia, to the city and to technology. What we are all thrashing around for is the inchoate pursuit of a gentler, simpler, more satisfying life. If the American Revolution transformed the world, what is going on in America today, beneath the spasms which are only the tips of the iceberg, will transform the meaning of life for an entire planet!

And that includes you, too. Forget that your back aches and you've lost your three sets of glasses. No matter. There is a place for the middle-aged in this revolution—the youth and the elderly have no monopoly. But we *do* have special problems and it is meet that the reefs and shoals be identified and that ways be charted to navigate the voyage with courage, calm and richness of spirit. This little book will help you to chart that course with dignity, or my name is not Philip Roth.

Many people think of middle age as the curtain scene, the last hurrah or the bottom line. Nonsense. Middle age is a time for regrouping. It is a time to catch one's breath (breath control is especially important for middle-agers) before the final assault on life's Mount Everest. Middle age is that exalted moment in life when miraculously, if we luck out, we get it all together. It is a time when we can still gain from our past mistakes, cast off in new directions, face new challenges. It is a time when we can savor the rich joys of yesteryear without getting mired in the past. It is the time when we become the sturdy bridge of several generations. It is the time when we are capable of perspective and focus, even if we *do* fall asleep in the middle of the page. It is the time when we are truly free, free at last. It is, in short, the time described by the bard which, when taken at the flood, leads on to drowning.

So don't knock it. Don't play it by ear. Don't be content with surviving it. Don't kvetch your way through it. Don't rush through it, briefcase akimbo, as if it were a commuter train. Savor it. Invest yourself in it. You have paid your dues; middle age can be the glorious payoff. In this blessed period arcing between acne and Leisure Village, between sunrise and sunset, you are Gary Cooper at the High Noon of your life, and middle age can give you more bang for a buck than any other of your several incarnations.

Now that you have happily found your way to this book you can enjoy the *flip side of your life!* So turn over, mate, you're better on the other side!

II

Consciousness-raising for the Middle Ages

One of the milestones of middle age is that under-whelming moment when your son or daughter reaches the age of independence. But when is That? How will you know it when he/she reaches it? It certainly is not graduation from high school or admission to college (because guess who is still paying the bills?) or even graduation from college (because, with your luck, he/she will linger on in graduate school for a terminal education). No, it is not connected with the calendar. It is a peculiar rite of passage and can happen at the most unexpected moment. This rite of passage to independence will be marked by one of the following:

(1) a long distance call from your youngster that will *not* be collect; or

(2) he or she will return your Shell credit card; or

(3) he or she is no longer a dependent on your income tax form.

YOUR KID IS NOW ON HIS OR HER OWN

It is important to know how to handle this radiant moment. Be cool. Do not make a fuss. You can set back the cause of independence by making a federal case out of what should be a lovely, understated moment. We know one parent who thundered into the telephone: "Hey, dummy! You forgot to tell the operator *collect*, so I'll have to mail you the $1.65 to pay for this call, it should only be three minutes!" And another parent, upon getting the credit card back, howled: "Listen, Sonny, you burned your draft card to protest the war, so how come you didn't burn the credit card to protest all that capitalistic materialism you put down all the time?" Such parental gaucheries are both petty and self-defeating. Accept the call, accept the credit card and, above all, accept his/her growing up. You have a choice?

IT'S THERE

You should keep your children and grandchildren in perspective (which is a college at least one thousand miles away from home). Children and grandchildren are the key to your middle age. If you have enough children (and grandchildren), you will have neither the time nor the energy to worry about yourself. To be a parent today you have to be committed (like to a mental institution). But we are not *only* parents, doomed to stand in the wings of life and watch our crazy kids perform on the center stage. We are *human beings, persons, adults in our own right,* and we should refuse to fade away like old soldiers. We should cherish

our dignity and humanity even when the prodigal
telephones us collect on Sunday evening, interrupting
the panel of rapists on the Susskind show just as the
raunchiest one is explaining that "You can't thread a
moving needle."

Father and Mother both get on the phone, beaming.
Hopefully they have an extension phone because that
makes it easier. The first three minutes rush by with
each of the parents asking the prodigal how she (or
he) is. Sandra says, "Okay," but neither parent is
satisfied either with the choice of word or the inflection
with which it is spoken.

"What's wrong?" they demand.

"Wrong? Who said anything was wrong? I said
everything is *okay.*"

"But whaddayamean *okay?* That's such a nothing
word," Father says.

"Sandra," Mother pleads, "tell the truth—is it that
guy from the fraternity . . . is that what's bugging
you? One of these rapesters on Susskind is pointy-
headed, just like him!"

"Look, I told you; I'm okay, I'm fine."

"Well, good, honey, did you hear about Aunt Shirley?" Father asks.

"Sam!" Mother barks darkly. "Why are you bringing
up Shirley?"

"What's wrong with Aunt Shirley?" Sandra wants
to know.

"Nothing. Nothing's wrong. What should be wrong?
She feels fine. Your father shouldn't have brought it
up, it's crazy."

"Why the hell shouldn't I bring it up? What's so
crazy about it?"

"Oh, Sam, it's not really important; we can tell her

in a letter. Why did you have to open your mouth and bring it all up?"

"Listen, Blanche, it's still a free country. I brought it up because I *wanted* to bring it up. Who died and made you the censor of the Bell Telephone system?"

"Who's censoring? Am I Spiro Agnew? But here we have a short conversation with Sandy, why does she have to hear about such a minor female tsoriss?"

"What's minor about a hysterectomy? I assure you Shirley doesn't think it's minor."

"Sam, I told you not to tell her. You had to start up."

"Mother, what's a hysterectomy anyway?"

"It's nothing. It's a woman's thing, nothing to it, like a female hernia, nothing."

"Hysterectomy? Mother, is that when a woman forgets her past?"

"No, Sandy, that's amnesia. Aunt Shirley doesn't forget anything, she has a memory like an elephant and she won't forget this either, Sam, you can bet your bottom. Of all things to bring up on the telephone to your baby!"

"Blanche, the baby is eighteen years old, she's old enough to be in college and if she's so backward she doesn't even know what a hysterectomy is, it's because you've sheltered her all her life."

"Sam, I didn't shelter. Maybe I guided; I helped; I didn't, God forbid, shelter. And what about you, you couldn't wait to lay a hysterectomy on her in the middle of a collect long-distance call on a quiet Sunday evening?"

"Listen, dear parents, I'm hanging up and you can finish this fight on your *own* time and as a *local* toll! I'm your daughter, remember, not a referee. And, please, don't call *me*. I'll call *you!*"

And the middle-aged parents continue the first real fight they've had in a long time—as a matter of fact, since Sandy's last call!

If you are truly adult, you will realize that the umbilical cord must be cut sometime, that you cannot seek to control your youngster forever and that there is no prouder moment than when he (or she) casts off the cocoon and takes off like a butterfly. So why are you crying, for pete's sake? There are no problems so big that you can't run away from them.

UP THE MIDDLE AGE

Speaking about kids, let THEM worry about US for a change. Why should we spend our lives worrying about whether Anthony will break a leg tripping over his own hair? Whether Claudia keeps a vaginal foam in her knapsack and will or will not wear a bra to the Family Circle meeting? Whether Harold will freeze to death in his sleeping bag in Vermont? And whether Heidi will soon run out of colleges to transfer to? We do not have to put *down* the youth culture. We have to *up* the middle ages! Let us no longer be lost between the youth people and the senior citizens. Leave us become our own force in America and be reborn in our individual lives. Enough being defined by our offspring. We, too, are real. Honest!

If the youth need to do their own thing, if blacks need to get themselves together, if senior citizens are becoming a political force to be reckoned with, if women need to have their consciousness raised, then dammit, now is the time for us middling, muddling middle-aged folk to get our heads together. Let us raise our consciousness before it is too late to get it up!

People growing into middle age are prone to depression. We imagine that we are declining, that the process of deterioration is at work like termites on both body and mental agility, that we are on the downward chute and that the best years of our lives are behind us. We are probably right, but that does not mean that we have to put our heads in the oven or waste ourselves on self-pity. What is needed is *mature self-acceptance*. True, we are no longer spring chickens, but we are not yet cold turkey, much less dead duck. The many years ahead can be adventurous and wondrous if we can *understand* and *accept* ourselves as we are. Maturity is the keynote and toward that end it is important that we raise our consciousness of ourselves as *mature* and *growing* human beings—and not as mere appendages to our children or as aging youths. A special sensitivity program on consciousness-raising for the middle-aged can perhaps help us in the task. . . .

Here, following, is an actual transcript of the first Middle-aged Consciousness-raising Session ever held:

LEADER: Now, the first question we have to face is: Who am I? Our lives are half over, maybe two thirds over and, sheet, we ought to begin to know who we are. Who wants to start?

FAYE: Me, I'll start. I am *me*. I know the correct usage is *I am I*, but what do you want, good grammar or good identity? ME! What is *me*? Until today, I would have identified this *me* as *mother* and *wife*. But, no, what good is that? After all, the kids are now grown up and even if they do not leave so soon, I'm sure as hell my husband will! So I have to find the

inner *me*, the internal *me* and the eternal *me*, which
I do believe I am now finding, thanks to the understanding heart of Tony the hairdresser.

CAL: I thought Tony was a fagele.

FAYE: I do not know what that word means, I am
not of that faith, but even if you're right, does that
mean he could not have an understanding heart, for
gosh sake?

LEADER: Of course, Faye. Who else would like to
express himself? How about you, Calvin?

CAL: I think I know who I am. I am an injustice
collector. I go around throughout my life, enjoying my
suffering. I am a modern-day Job. If it rains, it is
because the heavens are out to punish *me*! If my
daughter wins an abortion at the club raffle, it is all
a plot to embarrass *me*! I collect injustices the way
peddlers collect rags and trash. My personality is a
magnet for troubles, and my heart needs the suffering. So, believe it, in this world I am happy. That's
the real *me*.

LEADER: Thanks for that input, Cal. Let me ask you
people this: What should our relationship be with our
children after they have grown up and left home?

MIRIAM: What grown up? What left home? They
never do *either*! My thirty-two-year-old son, the bead-
maker, just split with his wife and where did he go?
You guessed it—home to Mommy! And my twenty-
eight-year-old daughter, the cobbler, has just taken
over our master bedroom because she says she needs
more privacy for her sex life. My husband and I have
built a bedroom and we're going batty in the belfry.
So where is it written that they grow up and leave
home? This is one of the myths perpetrated by the
media.

JOHN: I'm just talking off the top of my head, but I say that when the kids grow up they should be treated as autonomous, independent adults. Our relationship with them should be that of friends. You know . . . double dates, separate checks, the whole ball of wax. They should telephone first to see if it's convenient to drop in. Mutual respect, that's the ticket.

LEONARD: No way, John. And when the kids have kids, you'll be right back where you were at the beginning—baby-sitting, wiping their asses, buying the presents, worrying your head off. You'll learn that the sweetest sound on earth is the patter of little feet —going *out* of the house! The kids will telephone you first? You should live so long! The only answer is *distance*. My wife and I are moving to Australia and we'll thank you not to tell our kids.

FAYE: And, besides, Calvin, I resent your calling Tony a figaro, or whatever you said. Everyone is entitled to his own beliefs.

LEADER: And you, Jake, who are *you*? Don't censor your thoughts. . . . *React!*

JAKE: I'll tell you straight. Me, I'm an alta cocker. So what if you raise my consciousness? What for? Will it raise my income? My libido? My hair? My bowling score? Will it buy me a retirement home in Mexico? A young chick in Manhattan?

LEADER: So then why did you come to this consciousness-raising session?

JAKE: Who *came*? I *live* here! Rosie, my wife, invited *you*. I was supposed to go *bowling*. . . .

There are, of course, hundreds of techniques for raising consciousness. You can sit in a fishbowl. You can stand under a banner. You can swim around in a think tank. You can ride in a witch's cradle and have an ESP experience. You can find a middle-aged guru on a mountain. You can sit on the floor and rap with your friends. But the key question is: What do you *do* with your new-found consciousness *after* you have raised it? Once you get it up, what do you *do* with it?

As we have already noted, you can kvetch about your situation and that will offer some relief. But you must *also act!* Of course, once you fully understand your situation, you may have a tendency to *act* in a violent or self-destructive manner. You may, like many newly aware minorities, get furious as a shorn Samson and go running out of the house to pull down the columns of the temple. What if you internalize the rage? Well, you can jump off that bridge when you get to it. But that is not the way to go. Now that you understand the psychological and cultural bind of being middle-aged, you have to have the guts to take your little world in your hands and place it upon the anvil of life—and *beat it into better shape!*

So go find yourself a shrink.

III

Go Get Yourself a Shrink

Once you've reached your middle ages, it is awfully
late to start getting your brains unscrambled. What
have you been waiting for? After all this, why isn't
your head on straight? If you had started in your
teens, you could by now have run through the par-
for-the-course quota of four shrinks (Jungian, Ad-
lerian, Freudian and Herculean), spent a minimum
of $27,500 and four hopeful years in an orgone box,
had a quick but therapeutic affair with your last doctor
(who said: "I'm not sure this is good for *you*, but it
is very good for *me*" and added, in a burst of professional ethics, when you cried for a good-bye kiss:
"Look, I shouldn't even be here lying on the couch
with you!"). You could also, by now, have enrolled in
a wonderful encounter group in California where you
would have an opportunity to see yourself as others
see you ("What do I really think of you? You remind
me of a constipated cougar!"). By now you could definitely have been—well—still nutty, but strengthened
by that knowledge that you have gone the route,
knocked on every door, left no stone unturned, sub-

mitted your soul to every psychiatric guru you could
find in the Yellow Pages. You could enter the middle
ages preshrunk.

It wouldn't solve any of your *real* problems, but it
would be excellent table conversation, creating a circle
of like-minded friends and a way of life . . . if you
call this living. You would end up smart as ten colleges
and you might even have stopped smoking in the
process.

PRIMAL THERAPY

But since you failed to do all that, you have to play
psychiatric catch-up. You have to go right to the bottom
line. You have to go for broke. You can't putz
around with little insights, you need thunder-and-
lightning revelation. Perhaps, if you ascend the mountain, God will speak to you, but don't count on it,
you're an awful bore. So one daring, mind-blowing
experience remains possible: PRIMAL THERAPY!

My friend Manny Tsotskes went to the latest sensation in the psychiatric field, Dr. Finster Nacht, who
was just written up in *Reader's Digest* and whose
Nacht Primal Therapy patent is pending. Manny was
first interviewed by Dr. Nacht in the latter's walk-up
flat on the West Side of Manhattan ("Oh, how I hate
those bastards on the East Side," he said, opening the
conversation. "I would rather be mugged over here
than buggered over there."). At the conclusion of the
interview, Dr. Nacht put Manny in a room in a Howard
Johnson hotel where the telephone was disconnected,
the radio and television were shut off and for three
weeks Manny lay naked on the floor, forcing his memory back, back to his primal beginnings. During those

three weeks, Manny saw and talked to no one. He had no human contact whatsoever except for the little Puerto Rican attendant who slipped into the room in the middle of the night to give him his intravenous feeding of fried clams and to steal his credit cards. Otherwise, silence. Meditation. Floating back to his origins.

At the end of the three weeks, Dr. Nacht came to Manny's hotel room for the primal denouement. Gently, miraculously, he led Manny across the frontier of his very earliest memories: the agony of his first day in kindergarten; the delight he saw in his family's eyes when he toddled down the stairs at the age of three and sang to the startled guests at the dinner party, *"I wiped my tussy so carefully that now I am the ruler of the Queen's Naveee!"*; the time he was spanked for peeing into his little sister's farina. Manny lay on the rug, gasping and struggling, breaking through the blackness of memory, floating back to his own genesis.

"Farther," murmured Nacht. "You've got to go back farther, Manny."

Silence. Suddenly a shudder and a fierce shriek from the prone figure on the floor: *"Listen, you bearded sonofabitch, if you touch me one more time with that knife, I'll colecock you right here on the kitchen table!"*

Nacht beamed. "Your circumcision, Manny. Hmm, you don't *look* Jewish. Now just a few days farther back. C'mon, push, push!"

An hour later, his heart beating wildly, Manny reenacted his birth. Breast-stroking desperately in ambiotic fluid, afraid to emerge but unable to return to the warmth of his sanctuary, sensing a danger of strangulation, popping out like half a bagel from the toaster, Manny let out a cry that reverberated through the halls of Howard Johnson: "Oyyyyyy!"

"You made it, son," murmured Dr. Nacht. "You were born. You suffered. You are now reborn. You are now *you.*"

"Oh, thank God, Doctor," Manny said, lying exhausted on the rug. "Tell me, Doctor, all this traumatic primal digging, what does it all add up to?"

"It adds up to fifteen hundred dollars, Manny, not counting the fried clams."

DO IT BY MAIL

If primal therapy seems too intense and too steep for you, there is an easy way to get cheap help. Do it by correspondence. Don't bother with Ann Landers or Rose Franzblau, or the other self-appointed deities handing out platitudinous advice for the titillation of the mass public. Write directly to Dr. Finster Nacht (the same) who is, on the side, a specialist in the personal problems of middle age (and he charges by the word, not the hour). Here are some samples of private correspondence between Nacht and some middle-aged inquirers seeking confidential counsel.

＊　＊

Dear Dr. Nacht: Why am I so afraid of everything? Here I am, pushing forty, and I go around all day oozing fear and my sleep and dreams are also haunted by fear. So how can I work out I-Thou relationships when I'm afraid of everybody? Am I nuts?

(signed) FEARFUL

Dear Fearful: You think *you've* got problems! Listen, the real truth of middle age is that, behind the gray hair and the nice clothes and the Bar-Lev line psychological defenses, we are *all* still *little* boys and girls. I personally am just as afraid now as when I was a little boy. It is only the content of the fears that changes—and not always that, since I'm still scared shitless of heights, Poles, being embarrassed, breaking into a blush, plunging elevators, taking out the garbage at night. And now, as I get older, I also have the increasing fear of losing my virility (despite the nonsense which appears in Chapter VI). Frankly, Fearful, I'm afraid I can't help you, but it is good to get these things off your chest (or bosom; you don't identify your sex) and please send $22.50 (50 cents a word) and note the zip.

* *

Dear Dr. Nacht: Growing older is no big deal for me at all. I feel I am doing it gracefully. My only problem is that I am getting forgetful. My memory is like a sieve. Last week I went to a meeting of some young people, because contact with them keeps me youthful. I remember that I promised to do some work for this organization, but what the hell, I can't remember what organization or what I was supposed to do. (signed) FORGETFUL

Dear Forgetful: It was a meeting of the crazies and they blew up the local draft board without you. I hope the FBI is as forgetful as you. Don't forget to send $7.50; please do it now before it slips your mind.

* *

Dear Dr. Nacht: Last week I was mugged at high noon while praying in the fifth row of St. Patrick's Cathedral. That three hundred parishioners just kept

on praying while I yelled, "Jesus Christ, not here,
too!" doesn't bother me. Neither does the loss of my
money, watch, shoes and trousers. But they also took
a sheaf of incriminating love letters I got from my
mistress. What should I do?   (signed) NERVOUS

Dear Nervous: They will either blackmail you,
publish the letters in a paperback or steal your mistress. To me this really proves the inefficacy of prayer.

* *

Dear Dr. Nacht: I had a heart attack a few months
ago and I'm nervous about resuming sex relations. Of
course, I've asked my doctor, who says: "Yes, yes, if
you can climb stairs without strain you can certainly
get into the saddle." But how can I listen to him . . .
he just had a heart attack himself. So what say you?

(signed) CLIMBING STAIRS

Dear Climbing Stairs: You didn't say with WHOM.
Research shows that heart patients are prone to fatal
attacks during sexual relations in *extramarital* affairs.
Dr. Joseph B. Trainer has said that such affairs "tend
to raise the pulse beat and blood pressure above toler-
able levels." He also said we American males are "over-
weight, over-tobaccoed, over-alcoholed and undersexed." Based on Trainer, therefore, you obviously run
no risk of undue excitement if you resume sexual
relations with your own wife on the second floor at
home in an oxygen tent.

* *

Dear Dr. Nacht: I am impotent and proud of it.
Just as male homosexuals and lesbians are streaming
out of the closet and marching up Fifth Avenue demanding their rights in the Gay Liberation Movement,

so am I calling upon all closet impotents to stand up and be counted.

(signed) UNITED WE STAND, DIVIDED WE FALL

Dear UWSDWF: To be frank, I was wondering when a Paul Revere of the impotent movement would gallop onstage. You folks have been pitied, psychoanalyzed, denigrated, treated as basket cases by sexologists and written up long enough. You, too, have your rights, limp as they may be, and I salute your efforts. Needless to say, you have no way to go but UP!

* *

The dirty little secret is that, while shrinking is high-camp entertainment for us and remuneration for Dr. Nacht and all other shrinks, *we BECOME our parents in the end anyway.* You can shriek a lot, squirt venom and learn to hate your father (or mother) as the shrink helps you to realize that he (she) is to blame for everything wrong with you. But, at the bottom line, you will become *him* (*her*). We're all caught in the Saul-David syndrome. David saw Saul as a weary, ill, old man. Saul saw David as an excessively ambitious young man. When he became old, David became Saul. So it is with us. We spend a lifetime probing oedipal mysteries, thrashing to understand, to change, to grow, to free ourselves of that uncut parental umbilical, to become ourselves. And what happens? Look at a mirror. Look at your own children. You are traveling around in the very finest of circles. And so are your children and your children's children unto the umpteenth generation.

Meanwhile, stay loose and keep moving. A moving target is harder to hit.

IV

Exercise

This is one of the most vital chapters in the book. What can be more important than maintaining vigorous health through middle age? And how better to do that than through a regimen of bracing exercise? This chapter had intended to go into the merits of the Air Force exercise manual, water diet, Jack LaLanne Health Spas, shvitz baths and push-ups. However, in March of 1972, a prominent medical authority released a study (*Forum* magazine) showing that sexual activity is the best possible exercise, even for heart patients, that it involves all the muscles, releases thyroids, gets rid of tensions and tones up the middle-aged body real grand, like a motor tune-up job. So who needs this jogging jazz? Go right to Chapter VI on sex.

V

Parenthood Is Temporary,
So Become a Person Instead

As Shakespeare reminded us, all the world's a stage and we are actors playing various and shifting roles. Okay. What are the roles we middle-agers have to worry about? Bit parts!

It is natural for a parent to know how to relate to the kids when they are little. Feed them, diaper them, wash them, bug them and inject a little guilt into them . . . because that's what they grow on. Simple. But when they pass from adolescence into adultery, how do we relate to them? When they are too big to hit and too old for allowances (forty is too old for allowances), how do we get along with them (or without them) then? Shall we be buddy-buddy friends or continue to relate as parents and children? What do we do if they continue to need us and, worse, if they don't? These are good questions. I have some good answers, but they are NOT to *these* questions, everything notwithstanding to the contrary.

But what do you do when they grow up and stand on their own feet? One answer is, of course, break their legs so they will still need you, but sooner or later you must come to accept that they are adults, persons in their own right and they must make their own way in life. You have poured out your own lives for them—what have you stinted?—and now you have no right to demand anything, even gratitude, in return. In fact, it is easier to get the credit cards back than to get back gratitude, the mere suggestion of which arouses: "Why should I be grateful? Did I ask to be born?" Since there is no real answer to that one, drop it before they even begin to tell you the litany of how badly you scrambled their psyches in the first place.

But if not gratitude, at least respect, friendship? These things cannot be demanded either; they must be earned. It's partly a matter of personality, partly how much respect and trust you give them and—mostly— just luck. If you luck out, your kids may grow up to be your friends and maybe you'll go camping together once in a while, see a play or a movie, exchange books, go to the beach, enjoy each other's company. Otherwise, they'll go their way and you'll go yours and there's not much you can do about it.

No, you can't play the role of dominant parent all your life. Nothing is sadder than the parents who permit their lives to empty the moment the house becomes empty of the children. How sad—the father, who always played basketball and tennis with the kids, now rusting balefully in the den like an unrequited lover. And the mother suddenly facing an empty washing machine, a scary future and a blank-eyed husband who has become a morose attachment to the television set. How do you feel needed and useful when the young ones are gone—one to a distant college ("Tell me, you couldn't go to college around here?"), one to a commune where she is probably living with a bracero in a thatched hut along the Rio Grande, and one into marriage without conversion?

Well, the answer is you are still needed and useful! When parenthood becomes your entire life, you will either devour your young or they will fly the coop forever.

So bear in mind—*you need each other* if you are to make something out of the flip side of your life.

If you are the wife, shouldn't you see to it that hubby needs you? No doubt many of your girl friends have tried this whole bit—the sexy nightgown, the carelessly tossed copy of *The Sensuous Man,* the wine, the candlelight, the cleavage ("Honey, you'll catch cold"), the horny music, the whole shmeer. This is really the wrong route for you. In the first place, unless you check *TV Guide,* your little sexcapade is certain to be wiped out by the Super Bowl, the World Series, Johnny Carson or "All in the Family." Secondly, what if your little seduction really worked? What would you do for an encore? Do you want to exhaust your emotions and imagination playing the role of Scheherazade to Archie Bunker? And, besides, you should already have learned from your ungrateful kids that dependency is the wrong way to go. Be independent. Develop your own resources. Don't be a nudge all your life.

And you, the husband! What can you do to help get the two of you out of this funk and back on the track? First of all, *you* could answer the telephone once in a while; it wouldn't hurt. It's true that 98 per cent of the calls are still for the kids—it was even worse when the kids were *home* and three phones were going off con-

stantly like a central switchboard—and some of the calls
are long distance from their friends collect yet. Secondly, you could put down the newspaper, turn off the
television and just talk to her once in a while. Also, you
could help more around the house. You could dry the
dishes, walk the dog, pick up after yourself. You don't
have to be a jlob. These things together would not
mean a revolution, but they would be the beginning of
a better relationship. And, please, stop calling your wife
"Mom." She's your wife, not your mother, mate!

THE IMPOSSIBLE DREAM

But the most important thing is for each of you to
become a *person*. So maybe you should both go back
to school?

This is a capital idea. It will recharge your batteries.
It leads to much more self-development than mah-
jongg, much less guilt than having an affair (which you
could do if you didn't have to send roses next morning), and it will keep you young by keeping you in
touch with young people not your own (other people's
children are always *nice* kids). There is only one catch.
You will find that everyone else in college is also gray-
haired, middle-aged and searching for himself. The
young people, as you will discover, have all dropped
out or transferred out. College is no longer for the
young. It is for the reincarnated old, seeking rejuve-
nation. But, nonetheless, it will do you good so long as
you stay away from drugs, riots and group sex on campus. The husband can take night courses to stretch his
flabby mind. The wife can prepare herself for a profession. By the time of graduation, there will be quotas
for women as senators, astronauts, umpires, jockeys,

auto mechanics and marines. If you happen to be both black and female, you can almost name the corporation of which you want to be vice president. Hang in there. Soon you will be a person, an individual, a woman whose destiny is fulfilled. To your grown-up children you could mail your grades and term papers. To your husband you will be a success, an ornament or pride, a conversation piece . . . and a pain in the neck.

But, after you become a *person*, how will *that* affect your relationship with your grown-up kids?

It will make all the difference in the world. They will no longer see you as a household device, a human copy of Forever Yours, an object of their satisfaction who comes with the territory. No, indeed! They will come to see you as an adult, liberated, autonomous person and that will be an altogether new ball game. No more wistful Mommy holding a lantern at the window. No more sitting around the telephone each night waiting for son Davie or daughter Tracy to call. No more self-pitying letters which begin: "Would it hurt to pick up the telephone once a week, or even to put pen to paper so your mother wouldn't worry . . . ?"

No, now you will have your *own* life to lead, your *own* interests to pursue, your *own* inner vision to consummate. *Now*, when the children come home, the conversation will be *peer* to *peer*, talking head to talking head, as follows:

"Hi, there, Mom. You look just great!"

"Esther. You can call me Esther, Tracy."

"Oh, groovy, Mom! Say, what's to eat? I'm starved."

"In the freezer stands a roast beef. In the fridge one can find a salami, pate de fois and perhaps some wedges of cheese. Or, contrarywise, you might wish to telephone for take-out either Chinese, Italian, Chicken Delight or deli. Me, I'm off to school. Au revoir."

"You're a scream, Mom. We're so proud of you for going back to school. That's really a gas."

"Oh, speaking of gas, be sure to turn it off; your father is making tea. And don't forget to let him out before you go to bed."

"Just a minute, Mom, I mean Esther. I know you're into college and career and all that, but when am I going to have a chance to shoot the breeze with you like old times? I mean, don't you want to know about my work and about Clint and how much money we're making and all like that?"

"You can tell it to your father as soon as the commercial comes on. I really must run. It's been so pleasant seeing you again after all this time."

"*Mom, come off it! You're not* yourself! *It's me, Tracy, your favorite daughter. How can you treat me as if I were the stranger from the Welcome Wagon?*"

"Tracy, my dear, you must recognize the new reality. I cannot be Mother Earth forever. I'm now in a new stage. I'm in the process of *becoming.* I am now Esther . . . not Esther the obsolete mother, clutching a lost role, but Esther the *person,* the unique individual, moving ahead toward self-actualization. You must *accept* me on this new level of awareness, Tracy dear, do you understand? Can you *do* that?"

"I'll tell you the truth, Mom. I'm worried to death about you. Lately I can't sleep for worrying about you. I mean, what are you doing to yourself? Maybe you shouldn't have gone back to college. Maybe it's too hard for you. Maybe you and Dad should go away on a nice trip. Maybe you should go to the doctor and have a good examination."

And thus, presto, you will have achieved the impossible dream: *Role reversal*. Let your daughter be the *mother* for a change! Let HER worry about YOU! Now, thank heaven, you can lib it up in your middle age.

DIE WITH YOUR BOOTS ON

Despite the fact that we are merely aging juveniles, a basic rule of growing up is to *act your age*. There is nothing more pitiable than the middle-aged woman glued into a miniskirt aping her teen-aged daughter, or the father surrendered to fat and breathing like a fire truck, trying to wrestle with his teen-aged boys. Don't do it. Accept your age with grace and maturity. Die with your boots on.

The parent who persists in being a buddy to his grown child causes role confusion and stores up trouble for the future. One mother, who spent her life competing with her own daughter (using her clothes and make-up and vamping her boy friends) was finally told off by her child: "Fanny," she said, "I won't marry until I meet a guy who loves *me* and hates *you*."

As we have said, a constructive marriage can help keep your juvenile tendencies under check, particularly if you have married a truly adult mate who can redress your balances by gentle reminders, such as the following:

"Tell me, darling, I know it's an interesting hobby, but how long are you going to save old bottle caps?"

"Have you ever *listened* to yourself, dear?"

"Your diary is really so intriguing, honey, but do you think posterity will really care what you eat for dinner?"

"You are really a fine conversationalist, but you

would be even better if you could try thinking *before* you talk, dear."

"I am aware you are a Depression child, sweetheart, but must you continue to drop all the sugar packs and rolls into your bag every time we go to a restaurant, not to mention those damned doggy bags when we don't even have a *dog?*"

"Of course you have a right to drive in the drag races if that gives you pleasure, but those bubble-gum pictures of Willy Mays painted on the exterior of the Edsel look pretty silly."

What is the truly adult thing to do in every situation? Adult behavior—truly adult, that is—shows an awareness of your changing relationship to the world, a mature acceptance of evolving reality and coming to terms with the world and your developing position in it. Such mature understanding will make for a greater measure of satisfaction—if you don't panic and go right off the scope!

DEVELOP COMPATIBLE NEUROSES

"The rocks in my head fill the holes in yours." This epigram, used by Secretary of Commerce Peterson in 1972 to describe the relationship at that point in time between Richard Nixon and John Connally (*New Republic*, July 1, 1972), also has relevance to the arcane relations between husbands and wives. We're all a bit neurotic; it is only the richer among us who can afford to certify our psychic faults on the couch. The real coup is not to expurgate the neurosis—it probably can't be done without expending a king's ransom, if then, and your obsessive neatness would only come back as a sudden inability to ride elevators—so the best solution is to develop compatible and complementary neuroses

with your mate. Never mind about finances, educa-
tional achievements and common interests. Common
interests make for dull weather, and the key to how
you will make it as man and wife, now that you must
live for each other and not for the kids, is your inter-
locking hang-ups.

For example, let's say *you* tend to be indecisive. The
need to make a decision renders you unstuck. Well, if
your mate is a forceful, decisive type ("It's not *what*
you decide, but *that* you decide!"), you'll spend your
marriage in a towering rage of resentment. You'll feel
like an asterisk while he (or she) writes the book. No,
you're better off with an equally indecisive mate. That
way you can sit home together and engage in ever
closer togetherness.

"What should we do tonight, honey?"

"I don't know; what do you want to do?"

"Whatever you . . ."

"Well, if you want, we could go to a movie."

"Okay, if that's what you want. What'll we see?"

"No, I didn't say that's what I *want*. But if *you* want,
I wouldn't mind."

"Well, maybe. Or we could visit the Schillers. Her
mother died."

"If you want to. Or we could stay home and watch
TV—if we could decide what to watch, the game or
Carol Channing."

"Yeah, well, it's up to *you*."

"How come? It's up to *you*. I decided last night."

"Last night we didn't do anything, remember? We
couldn't decide whether to go for a ride or walk out
and get some ice cream."

"Look, it's not easy to decide."

"No, it *looks* easy, but it's really not."

"I know. Let's ask somebody over for ice cream."

"Okay, but whom . . . and what flavor?"

"Whom do you want?"

"I dunno. Whom do you?"

"Oh, the water's boiled. Tea or coffee?"

"I don't care . . . whatever you . . ."

This couple doesn't do much, but they are tied closely and tenderly together by an umbilical cord of indecisiveness. It may seem, from the outside, that their wheels are always spinning. True, but it's *one* vehicle, they are mired together, and they are never at a loss for conversation, which is more than you can say about your model couple, glistening in their common interests, driving home from their beloved opera in total silence.

Or let's say you are one of those persons who makes lists. Let's hope you are not married to another list maker. The prospect of separate but equal lists raises the specter of familial chaos. It would also result in untoward competitiveness. Did you notice my list is longer than yours? How come you didn't list buying stamps? Do I have to think of everything? I happened to look at your list and I think it's ridiculous to put down: "Take a bath." No, in dealing with this kind of neurosis, you need a mate with a neurosis which will complement yours.

There is another middle-aged couple of my acquaintance who are long on lists, but they too have saving complementary neuroses. Helen is a compulsive list maker. Henry, editor of a chain of comic magazines, edits the list. And Helen, brilliantly canceling out one neurosis with another, then proceeds to lose the list. In this household, too, the creative interaction of diverse neuroses makes for closeness—call it healthy mental illness, if you wish.

"Darling," Helen says. "I made a list of things to be done tomorrow."

"Good," says Henry. "Lemme look at it." Snatching the list, Henry whips through it, correcting the spelling here, striking redundancies there ("Why do you have to say '*talk* to Timmy's teacher?' What else are you going to do but *talk?* Are you going to mau mau her? Just say 'Timmy's teacher.' And why did you put down 'Call Uncle Fred?' He'll invite himself to dinner. I'm striking that! The rest is okay.")

"So give me the list; I'll put it in my purse so I won't forget it."

"Where is your purse?"

"What? It must be here; I just had it when I went shopping. Did you see it?"

"No, you must have left it at the store again."

"I'll run to the store and get it. Give me the list; I'll do the grocery things at the same time. It shouldn't be a total loss."

So Helen runs to the store (she runs by car) to recover her purse again and, laughing uproariously at herself in conversation with the cashier, unconsciously drops the new list into a passing market basket, thus obviating the headache of carrying out the foolish hassles which she and her husband had so happily co-authored. It's no wonder that Henry and Helen enjoy their lives together—like Gilbert and Sullivan, they have a little list, but unlike Henry's secretary, who lists as a result of a gigantic bosom, they don't get unbalanced in the process.

MACROBIOTICS . . .

Complementary neuroses have their counterpart in the philosophy of macrobiotics (an ancient diet). The idea is that the universe (like marriage) functions by the interplay of opposing but complementary forces. Yin, which is typically female, tends toward expansion. Yang, which is typically male, tends toward contraction. Thus, according to the founding fathers of macrobiotics, the quality of life is greatly enhanced when a dietary balance is achieved between Yin and Yang. In addition, to the correct Yin-Yang ratio, proper chewing is also essential. Thus, even in eating, complementary neuroses can help buck up your sagging marriage. If your wife is into macrobiotics, while she is chewing her unpolished rice seventy-five times you will have plenty of time to do the dishes, dust the furniture, walk the dog and hiss the President on the Cronkite program. If you are the one bugged by macrobiotics (you can catch it from your kids, like insanity), remember that it can prolong your life anywhere from ten to fifteen years, provided only that you do not drop dead (chewing all the while) from sheer starvation.

AND/OR SEX

And, of course, complementary neuroses have to do with sex as well. One would imagine that it would be best for an oversexed woman to marry a similarly souped-up man. On the contrary. Such a relationship has a specious and spurious allure, but in actual practice it does not cut the mustard. What is "oversexed," anyway? It's a relative matter, and in general it is relative to the habits of one's own mate. A person secretly relishes considering herself (or himself) "oversexed," but one can only get away with this self-aggrandizement if one's mate is less sexed than one's self. How do you consider yourself an oversexed creature if your mate beats you to the sack nine times out of ten? Such zeal is neither fair nor helpful.

No, to maintain one's self-image as oversexed or undersexed, one should marry a mate who is the opposite. This permits each mate to feel a minimum of hearty resentment, thus justifying healthy fantasies about other partners as well as introducing a needed ingredient of spiritual tension into a relationship which would otherwise be wholly athletic and acrobatic.

Sex is vital to the development of personality and marital relations, but sexual differences are also crucial. It is no good if both partners are undersexed, either, unless they are the first couple (indecisive) described above. They would have to sit down and decide where they stand whenever they go to bed together. Differing sexual rhythms are helpful. They introduce suspense, mystery, tension and unpredictability into the couple's sex life. Sex, like foreign policy, requires unpredictability if it is to maintain its credibility. What will happen tonight? A gas or just gas on the stomach? This question, quickening the blood, has no point if we are talking about two nymphomaniacs or two frigid mackerels. A well-modulated marriage combines two different rheostats, keenly tuned to two different temperatures, converging in the unexpected accommodations of the marital bed.

Besides, nymphomaniacs are not so easy to come by.

THE VORSPAN RULE

Once you understand the Vorspan rule of Complementary Neuroses, you begin to understand the hidden dynamic of marriage. Thus, most couples who seem to be miserable together are really enjoying their misery.

I mean, why did they find each other in the first place and what keeps them together now? In marriage, as in life, we get what we deserve—our lumps. It comes with the territory.

You look at a couple and you wonder: Of all the souls on earth, how did these two get together? Why them? So peculiar a match. He a cretin, she an Amazon. What could they possibly see in each other? Simple . . . a psychological response to a deep-running inner need. He needs to be a bastard and she needs to be bastardized, he needs to be a lion and she needs to lionize. In most cases, the liberated woman has merely found an updated version of her own father (or, for the same reason, his very antithesis). And her husband, after all his years of analysis, has simply found a surrogate mother. Nobody admits it, but watch the contour of the husband-wife relationship and you'll see re-enacted the particularities of each mate's original relationship with his (her) parents.

Example: Blanche as a child had been scared to death of her father, whom she nonetheless loved very much. When he lost his temper, his voice would boomingly break the sound barrier throughout the house. Blanche, as a child, would hide under her bed until the volcano was over. Now, in adulthood, Blanche has married a trigger-happy Harry who flies off the handle at a moment's notice. Blanche has been married to Harry for ten memorable years—five *on* and five *under* the bed, thus shlepping her formative years right into maturity. We do not escape our childhood or our parents; we merely re-enact the scene in our marriage!

Or take Luke. As a child, Luke was happy-go-lucky, but whenever his mother would rebuke him he would retreat into a sullen silence that could last for hours.

Now, at thirty-five, Luke is married to a sweet, easy-going woman named Sandra. Sandra is devoted to Luke, but she can't understand why it is that if she says, "Darling, did you have to start eating before the hostess even sat down?" Luke will automatically go blank for a week. What seems strange to Sandra after all these years was perfectly manifest to Sandra's cagey old mother-in-law thirty years ago: "If you look cross-eyed at that kid, he becomes a silent movie."

The more things change, the more they are the same. Age sophisticates and camouflages our childish hang-ups, but only the grave obliterates them. We grow *old,* more than *up!*

YOU TALK TOO MUCH

Growing up requires inner peace. And in these days of noise pollution and the crushing rat race, it is essential to cultivate moments of privacy and peace. We have come to a sad pass when so many people can't stand themselves without a radio, television or friend blaring. These psychological basket cases can't feel alive unless they hear the outside world blasting their ears. We all know people who virtually tremble if forced to spend some time alone. Herdlike, they must flee their aloneness and huddle against other human beings, including strangers, for mutual warmth. Healthy human relationships are crucial to the process of maturing—growing up—but dependency is a curse, and occasional moments of silence bring nourishing shade and calm into the fever of daily life.

Mr. and Mrs. Pierce A. Beam of St. Martin's, Maryland, celebrated their seventy-sixth wedding anniversary in 1972. Mr. Beam, one hundred, was asked by a reporter how he and his wife, Della, ninety-two, were getting along after three quarters of a century. "Oh," he said, "we don't fuss much any more, we can't hear each other." Perhaps if Eve hadn't heard Adam say, "Listen, we live in an age of transition," the whole history of mankind might have been brighter!

Silence may not be golden, but it is vital to mental health. Our children spend more hours in front of the television set than they do in the classroom. And we, their parents and grandparents? We also watch too much, talk too much, rush too much. So let's institute a very simple regimen to humanize our lives. Most of us spend ten or fifteen minutes in calisthenics before going to bed and/or upon arising. Well, considering how little that has done for us, as an unsparing look at the full-length mirror will testify, why not replace that frantic wagging of limbs with ten minutes of daily *silence?* No radio, no television, no hollering at the kids, no making of silly lists, no conversation. Just silence.

If you have a garden or forest or mountain at hand, great! Otherwise, just go out on the back porch and sit quietly. It would be best to walk the dog first, lest the ten minutes be filled with suggestions from your loved ones that it's your day to walk Kelev, your unquiet dog. Once the dog is out of the way, however, you can sink into your meditation. Force yourself not to think about the upcoming trials of the day or the irritations of yesterday. Flush your mind and let the quiet wash your brain. If your nosy neighbor tries to engage you in conversation as he goes out to pick up the paper, ignore him. Concentrate on nothingness, renew yourself with silence and tame the stormy waters of your soul. Sha, already!

WHAT ENDURES?

So, if parenthood is temporary, let's admit that nowadays marriage is, too. Almost one out of every two marriages now ends in divorce or a "Yankee" trade, and the latest rage is divorce insurance. Naturally, we can't follow statistics too slavishly. A WASPish New Yorker friend of mine got all uptight when he was told by his wife that she was pregnant with their fourth child. He had just read that every fourth child born in New York City is Puerto Rican. Yet marriage *has* become a precarious, vulnerable institution. The pressures of our time, including the women's lib revolution, require the marriage partners to be flexible, to be co-operative and—especially—to chart new and humane sex roles (not the artificial ones imposed by the society) if marriage is to survive.

The drudgery of the household should no longer be assumed to be the obligatory province of the woman. The household tasks should be divided up, co-operatively and equally as is already being done by one model couple, as the following vignette suggests:

HIM: Let's have some coffee, okay?

HER: Good. You boil the water; I'll put the Nescafé in the cups; you get the saucers.

HIM: Okay, I'll bring in the milk and the sugar; you bring in the silverware.

HER: I'll bring in the pound cake; you bring in the Dutch apple pie.

HIM: I'll slice, if you'll bring in the pie dishes.

HER: I'll bring in the pie dishes if you'll clear afterward.

HIM: I'll clear afterward if you'll wash the dishes.

HER: I'll wash if you'll dry. Who'll stash away?
Pause.

HIM AND HER (*together*): Listen, let's forget the whole scene and watch TV.

If parenthood is temporary (it says here), and even marriage may be transitory, what endures is PERSONHOOD. To be an adult person, to stand upright with your head in the stars and your feet on the ground, to be *no one's toy thing* or crutch, to be alive while still living, to grow wiser and gentler with the years—those are the dimensions of personhood, although they seem more like the impossible dream. Such a PERSON will be unshakable and unflappable. Let son number one call from Dartmouth to announce he is leaving college to live in the woods and become a woodcutter. No matter. Let daughter number one, who teaches Indian lore at a Jewish camp, write and say she has been attacked by a violent religious fanatic who carved a menorah with a stylus on her back. No matter. It could have been worse; it could have been the Ten Commandments or Deuteronomy 23. Let son number two get picked up for smoking dope with the village narc who had cajoled him with: "Light up—or *Get off the pot!*" No matter. Let daughter number two get into so much trouble that she gives the idea of infanticide a good name. No matter. Let your own lifemate leave you to live with a bouncing beach boy in Majorca. Sad, but still not the end of the world.

You are still *you*, an inviolable and enduring human being. They can't take *that* away from you. You still have your own self, your own life—if you can call that living.

VI

Ten Steps to a Swinging Sex Life

One of the keys to middle-aged happiness is your sex life. There are lots of young blatherskites who think we have had it when it comes to sex. Dr. Harold Lear cites a study in which young people were asked to complete the sentence, "Sex for older people is . . ." Most college students finished the sentence with the words, "unimportant," "negligible" and "passed."

What do *they* know? The truth is that sex is largely wasted on youth; it might even be too good for them. For us, on the other hand, it improves from year to year, like old wine if you just keep your bouquet sharp. As we will shortly demonstrate, you can ball right into your eighties if you play the game right.

Those weary souls who say that sex is a thing of the past for us middle-agers are dead—and the dead should not counsel the living. The truth is that middle age is the ideal stage of life for marital fulfillment and sexual

enrichment. The early fumbling years of marital trial-
and-error adjustment are over. The kids are grown up
and away at college. The telephone and stereo do not
roar as incessantly as before. The stream of barefoot
young strangers pouring through the house enroute to
the refrigerator, like locusts, has ebbed. Preparing
meals is no longer a big-time consuming hassle—how
long does it take to cook two eggs and pull two yogurts
out of the refrigerator? The house is quieter, the beat is
softer, Mozart has replaced the Fugs on the record
player, the fireplace glows softly and in the evening
there is time for a cocktail while gently sharing the
experiences of the day. With all this privacy and
tenderness pervading the house, and with those college
bills knocking out all other forms of entertainment,
what are you going to do? Make out the bills?

1. The key to healthy and satisfying sex in middle
years is *spontaneity*. The carefully planned and rit-
ualized sexual regimen is a bummer. Now, for the first
time, you can respond when the spirit moves you. It's
a mechiah! This does not mean you have to be crazy
like the spontaneous couple who were barred from
Reuben's restaurant for life, or the couple who got
ardent on the Verrazzano Bridge and knocked out the
exact change lane.

True, spontaneity can sometimes boomerang. The
newspaper recently brought us the tale of the couple
with the troublesome car which was always breaking
down and with which the husband was always tinker-
ing. One day the wife came home from shopping and
saw what she thought was the familiar sight of her
husband's legs protruding from beneath their car once
again. Playfully, she reached under the car and, fon-
dling, said: "Ding dong, darling, Mommy's home."

Then she proceeded into the house to find—you guessed it—her husband drinking coffee at the kitchen table, while the local mechanic lay under the car cold as a mackerel, having knocked his shocked head against the underside of the car.

2. *Look Young.* Modern technology has made it unnecessary for you to look so seedy. "Staying beautiful, even at age thirty-six, is a snap," according to Princess Luciana Pignatelli, a beauty consultant quoted in the New York *Times.* In her own case, she reported, it's the simplest of matters. She remains beautiful, she says, because (a) she had a nose operation; (b) she takes periodic liver injections; (c) she has her eyelids operated on at intervals; (d) she takes daily yoga exercises for her figure; (e) she takes silicone injections beneath each cheekbone to smooth out crow's-feet. "See . . . anybody can stay beautiful," the interviewer concluded. "It's just a matter of putting it all together!"

So why do you sit there looking like such a wreck? Get rid of that pince-nez and insert contact lenses. Why do you have such buck teeth? Write to Pepsodent for bright new caps. If you are a female, get a blond wig. If you are a male, write to the CIA and order a red crew-cut rug, but do not wear it during espionage, swimming and/or sex. Always sport a suntan which can conceal any disease, like papering over the crumbling wall, even though under that tan you're pale. Get a new wardrobe so you look like Harry Belafonte with a black shirt open to the navel. Don't be a stick-in-the-mud. If necessary, change your nose, your name and your luck. Because looking good is the name of the game and if *you* can have a swinging sex life, anybody can!

3. *Don't Smoke So Much.* The Russians, who have

invented and discovered everything in sight, have now announced that heavy smoking can make middle-aged men lose interest in sex. The Soviet newspaper *Sovietskaya Rossiya* reported there was scientific evidence that smoking lessens sexual activities of men forty years old and older, or even as young as thirty. "One reason for this," the newspaper said, "is changes in the blood which produces changes in sex hormones."

Well, maybe that's true of RUSSIANS, but we have our doubts if it applies to good, red-blooded AMERICANS. If, perchance, it *did* apply to us, it would certainly drive the last nail in the coffin of Marlboros and Camels. That cigarettes cause cancer has not bothered American cigarette addicts too much. But if it wipes out our sex life, that's un-American.

4. *Show Emotion.* Dr. Charles W. Peek, of the University of Georgia, thinks American men don't have what it takes to cut the sexual mustard because we grow up with the John Wayne-James Bond syndrome that a man should be strong, silent, unfeeling, afraid to express emotions, treating women "with an air of emotional detachment and independence." Dr. Peek added: "As the cowboy equally loved his girl friend and his horse, so the present-day American male loves his car or motorcycle and his girl friend. Basic to both these descriptions is the notion that the cowboy does have feeling for women but does not express them since, ironically, such expression would conflict with his image of what a male is."

Dr. Peek is libeling the American male. No feelings? Has Dr. Peek ever peeked at an American male watching the Super Bowl or the World Series on television? What a flood of natural emotion—anger, exultation, rage, tenderness, affection! It is quixotic to expect the

American male to surrender his horse, his motorcycle, his girl friend or his television set. Why not encourage him instead to make love on the horse and the motorcycle as he used to do in the back of the car until he slipped his disc? And, instead of proclaiming themselves weekend widows and storming out of the house when the games go on, why shouldn't the American wife tap into this flood of genuine emotions and seduce her husband at half time and perhaps during those long commercials for Noxzema Shaving Cream and Alka-Seltzer? Try it; you'll like it!

5. *Beware of the twenty-one-year itch.* Our movies and other media, bewitched by youth, make a big thing of the seven-year itch. This is held out as a sensitive watershed when the young wife and husband develop restless and roaming eyes and when dalliance sometimes ensues. But let it be said here and now that the so-called seven-year itch is an evanescent tickle compared to the twenty-one-year itch, which is less an itch than a time bomb hot to trot!

You all know the symptoms. Not only the roving eye, the dancing blood, the cold showers. The ultimate symptom is when you and your wife suddenly can't make it because neither of you can think of anyone to *fantasize* about. That, my friend, is the twenty-one-year itch, and it can keep itching all the way to the grave.

But the big question is: What do you do about it? What *can* you do about it?

Well, you can feel guilty about your feelings, and you can go out and sublimate them. You can go on an ecology kick and pick up empty beer cans and pop bottles. You can go to the local political club and volunteer to lick envelopes or Democrats. You can go to your local church and volunteer to make damp tuna

sandwiches for the annual brotherhood luncheon. You
can short-sheet the kids' beds. You can take up yoga or
learn parachute jumping. You can join the local de-
cency league and spend your time monitoring dirty
movies. You can write a novel, acting out all your
fantasies, entitled "I Was a Philanderer for the FBI."
But, truly, it won't wash. You still itch.

Then, what is to be done? One way is to take up
the slack with a lover on the side, but there are the
following problems: (1) Where, pray tell, are *you* going to find a lover? (2) Even if you could, where could
you find the loot for a hotel room, particularly since
your mate controls the family bread? And with your
slipped disc, forget about the Volkswagen. (3) You're
such an inept liar that you would no doubt rush home
at midnight and breathlessly exclaim to your waiting
spouse: "You'll never guess where *I've* been tonight!"
(4) You might get a certain pleasure out of the ar-
rangement, but it would drive you out of your head if
you thought your mate had gone and done likewise, because you are an itchy male chauvinist pig at heart.

The only effective way to hack the twenty-one-year
itch is to confront your loving wife, talk things through
honestly and work out your problems together. As follows:

HUSBAND: Darling, there's something I've been want-
ing to talk to you about.

WIFE (*washing dishes*): So talk!

HUSBAND: No, it's something—well, personal, about
us. Can't we at least sit down?

WIFE: When I finish, I'll sit. Meantime, you want to
talk to me, why can't you dry the dishes, it wouldn't
hurt, we could stand and talk?

HUSBAND: All right, already. Give me the dish towel and I'll dry.

WIFE: Use two hands, please. All I need is you should drop my best china.

HUSBAND: If Nixon could do it, I could do it (*big guffaw*). Listen, I have to talk to you. You know, we're now married twenty-one years and this year is, I don't know if you know it, a milestone in our lives.

WIFE: What milestone? Twenty is copper, twenty-five is silver, fifty is gold, what is twenty-one?

HUSBAND: Twenty-one is ITCH.

WIFE: Whaddayamean ITCH?

HUSBAND: How should I explain? It has been proved that on the twenty-first anniversary, give or take a little, both parties to a marriage get a little . . . a little . . . a little . . .

WIFE: I know, I know. But when we were married only ten years, did we get any more? You'll drop my cup!

HUSBAND: No, that's not it. I mean, after all, after twenty-one years you begin to take each other for granted, you know, no big surprises after all, you know what you got, and sometimes things get a bit boring—

WIFE: Tell me, you're talking sexually?

HUSBAND: Well, yes, sexually, too.

WIFE: Then, if that's the case, mister, I have some big news for you. Today I went to a consciousness-raising meeting and I became a Woman's Libber and I now understand that *my body belongs to me*. Not to Mr. Nixon or to Teddy Kennedy, it's not the government's business, and not to any other male chauvinist pig, including *you*. So you want to share my *body*, which belongs only to me, you will also share with the child-rearing and with the housework headaches which now belong equally to us both! If you would prefer a marriage contract which will put this into writing, fine. Otherwise, I'm very sorry about your *itch*, but we can stop it only if we start altogether from *scratch*.

HUSBAND: I just dropped my cup!

As well as the whole goddam conversation!

6. *Enjoy, enjoy.* And, if you are faithful to the foregoing advice, here is the best news of all. You can look forward to a rich, vital sex life into ripe old age. We have it on the authority of Simone de Beauvoir, writing in *Harper's* in January 1972, that "the happier and richer sexual life has been, the longer it goes on." She tells us of the famous Duc de Richelieu's father, who "married for the third time in 1702 at the age of seventy. When his son was sixty-two and governor of Guinne, he led a life of debauchery. In his old age, he seduced a great many young women. At seventy-eight, bewigged, made-up and very thin, he was said to look like a tortoise thrusting his head out of its shell; this did not prevent him from having affairs with the actresses of the Comédie-Française. He had an acknowledged mistress, and he spent his evenings with whores; sometimes he used to bring them home—he liked listening to their confidences. He married when he was eighty-four and had recourse to aphrodisiacs; he made his wife pregnant. Furthermore, he deceived her, too. He continued his sexual activities right up until his death at the age of ninety-two."

Mme. de Beauvoir reminds us of such elderly fellows as Charlie Chaplin, Picasso, Casals, Henry Miller and Bernard Berenson who, before he died at the age of ninety-four, wrote: "I only really became aware of sex and of women's physical, animal life at the period that might be called my old age."

If men's sexuality is not greatly affected by age, a woman goes on forever. De Beauvoir quotes Brantome as saying that a woman "at no matter what age is endowed with, as it were, a furnace . . . all fire and fuel within." Kinsey found that when women are sixty, their capacity for pleasure and sexual desire is the same as it was at thirty. De Beauvoir reports that when Andree Martinerie was conducting a study for *Elle* magazine (March 1969), she garnered some fascinating confidences from elderly women. Madame F., a rich, middle-class sixty-eight-year-old, a militant Catholic, mother of five and grandmother of ten, told her, "I was already sixty-four. . . . Now just listen: four months after my husband's death I went down into the street just like someone who is going to commit suicide. I had made up my mind to give myself to the very first man who would have me. Nobody wanted me. So I went home again."

Not only does the sacred fire not burn out with age, but the libido maintains an unbroken link to creativity. Here is De Beauvoir quoting the aged Gide: "There was a time when I was cruelly tormented, indeed obsessed by desire, and I prayed, 'Oh, let the moment come when my subjugated flesh will allow me to give myself entirely to . . . But to what? To art? To pure thought? To God? How ignorant I was! How mad! It was the same as believing that the flame would burn brighter in a lamp with no oil left. If it were abstract, my thought would go out; even today it is my carnal self that feeds the flame, and now I pray that I may retain carnal desire until I die."

What does this all mean? It means today is the first day of the rest of your life. It means your sex life is like a child's swing. It can just rust there. Or, if you

wish, you can push it, get it up and take off on a swinging sex life.

Now let's face it, the incompatibility in your marriage has nothing to do with sex anyway. If you continue to sit like a zombie watching every sports contest
while your wife wants to listen to Beethoven, your
marriage will go right down the drain. The solution is
simple. Either have two television sets—His and Hers—
or take protective reaction. Learn to watch football
with the volume off and put a Mozart record on the
stereo to keep your wife happy. I have a friend who has
been doing this for so long he has developed a Pavlov-
ian reaction—he rolls on the floor and screams silently
while his wife reads a book and listens to the opera.
If this system makes you a little weird, get a television
set with an ear plug so you and your wife can function
together without killing each other. This is the best
way to be away from home while still being home.

7. Also, marriage counselors have taught us that
husbands and wives *should not have lunch home together* during the week. It results in resentment for
the wife and yogurt for the husband. Seventy per cent
of the wives whose husbands come home for lunch
during the week have gone over the hill, 20 per cent
have been driven to the sewing circle or the PTA and
10 per cent have gone on diets which preclude lunch.
If you have retired or been fired, don't let your wife
know. Spend each day in the park, eat hot dogs, fly a
kite and work up an appetite and come home for dinner at the usual time. The marriage you save may be
your own.

8. Occasional *separate vacations* are a good idea.
Too much togetherness can smother a relationship.

Each of you should take a long trip alone once in a while, and you'll love each other even more.

What happens in separate vacations is that the first week you're apart you delight in the separation and spend the time going out and "rediscovering yourself." The second week you eat a lot of TV dinners, wax nostalgic, forget what it was about him (or her) that used to drive you up the wall. The third week you begin to sigh over snapshots of your missing mate, write adoring letters and whistle all the old familiar songs the two of you used to dance to (like "Mairzy Doats" and "It's Only a Paper Moon"). During the fourth week, your entire married life passes in review before your eyes, like a rerun of "An American Family," and you realize that, in your relationship with your spouse, while you may have been *wrong*, you were *never* in doubt.

After five weeks you are—once again—madly in love with your mate and you maintain that exalted pitch of passion until the very moment you see him (or her) at the airport, suntanned and beaming that obnoxious grin all over the terminal. You'll drive home in silence, so plan another separate vacation quickly so that you can fall in love once more.

IF NECESSARY, TAKE IT IN FOR REPAIRS

Now and then, of course, something may develop— illness, enforced separation, NFL playoffs, going into a nunnery on early admissions—which may force an interruption of your normal sex life for weeks or even months at a time. Try shifting gears. Do not fall for the myth that abstinence makes the heart go fonder. Abstinence, at your age, can make you forget which end is up. Sex, after all, is not necessarily a skill you remember forever, like riding a bicycle. After a long layoff, you could easily fall off.

So, therefore, if you begin to fall off regularly, go in for repairs. The ideal neighborhood service station is Masta and Baders, which gives you a twelve-month warranty or ten thousand miles, whichever occurs first. Masta and Baders provide surrogate husbands and wives as well as the best in technological equipment, including a pornograph, Hegar dilators and a brown paper bag to cover the face of the less-attractive partner. Here, in the privacy of Masta and Baders television camera, you will learn sexual athletics on the high wire, the mat, the gymnastic horse and the sliding pond. You will learn the erogenous, dmz and business zones of sex-on-demand. You will learn how to adjust the mirrors, the light, the pillows and the paper moon. You will learn the mechanical joys of automated sex play. Your body will become an Erector Set, and you will have more outlets than the local electrician.

Maybe you are not cut out for fancy sex. But, please, at least stop pounding your chest and asking, "How was I?"

USE STIMULANTS

As you get older, you should not be reluctant to make use of whatever mild stimulant heightens your sexual anticipation and ardor. Maybe screening a sex flick will turn you on; then let it roll. Maybe a belt of scotch will do the trick. Perhaps reading the Song of Songs together will heat things up. It may be that lighting up a joint, however illegal, will sharpen your sensitivities. Sex, like smoking, is okay for consenting adults in private. Whatever pleases you, without harming anybody, is appropriate. If it turns out to be strobe lights, running water, the Johnny Carson show, the Red Army chorus, Howard Cosell, hammocks suspended from the chandelier, *The Thirty-nine Steps,* a magic carpet, sunset at Jones Beach, sunrise on the Golden Gate, a Holy Roller meeting, getting your hands on a Toyota, joining the airline's Mile High Club, yoga or Fuyu-Nu-Yu pottery —don't scruple. You are not a dirty old man; you're just a sexy mature citizen.

But just remember that, despite Masta and Bader and other mechanics, the best stimulant is still the oldest. It's LOVE. Love makes the world go round and, despite all the poor-mouthing of our day, TLC (tender loving care) is still the only sure-fire fuel which can send your sexual rocket up and away into outer space.

VII

Finding Entertainment

Elsewhere in this crisp volume, we (what's with this *we* bit? This book is written by one crotchety fellow grimly fighting middle age) cite the importance of exercise—physical exercise—and hobbies that will involve you in doing things with your hands. However, let's be realistic. Knowing you, you'll find damn good reasons not to take that route. Instead, you'll continue to rust on your laurels, seeking entertainment as a passive spectator immobilized plop in front of the movie screen, the stage, the boob tube and—maybe—the opera house. In each of these, however, there are vital rules to follow, as follows:

THE MOVIES

Virtually every movie you see will be a "youth scene" pic. This is because (a) that's all they make any more; (b) the only one-dollar movie house in the neighborhood is run by a bearded youth who, on principle, shows no movies about anyone over thirty; and (c) you are one of those parents who tries to understand, saying, "Listen, maybe they're right."

In every such movie, Elliot Gould will be an over-age student commuting between flaming campus riots and a quick roll in the hay with a wan blonde who is married to a history professor who gets his jollies from the Boy Scouts. Like most middle-aged people, you will enjoy the boffo sex scenes at first, but after a while you will get tired of that mop of hair on Gould's chest and all the grunting and wheezing (a cross between passion and asthma) and you will grow nostalgic for the good old movies when the sexual act was merely suggested, right after the sweet caress, by a view of the sun dappling the swaying trees or the gentle Irish mist falling on the mountains. Bear with the sex and violence because these movies are good for your soul. They gratify your masochism. They are designed to show what shits we are, we adults who have mucked up this world for the innocent children. Try to remember that the foppish professor, who sells out his students; the priggish president, who sells out his college to the FBI; and the homosexual coach, who arranges for the basketball star to cuckold him; and the Dagwood Bumstead father, who gets falling down drunk while looking for his daughter who has wisely run away from suburban affluence—*all these are us!* So enjoy!

Youth movies are mostly lousy movies, but they are very important to help us middle-agers *understand* the young. Having sat through dozens of these Elliot Gould youth flicks, I think I am beginning to *understand*. These films hold themselves out to be mirrors of our time, reflecting with sharp accuracy the violence, the racism, the ugliness and the plastic emptiness of

our (read non-youth) lives. But it is a put-on. They
are not *mirrors* at all. They are *shapers* of the very values they pretend to mirror. The real world is sorry
enough, no question, but the youth movie world is a
special brand of nightmare produced by middle-aged
sycophants of youth to zing *us!* And this world of fantasy has its own set of values: Life is cheap, man stinks,
living has no purpose, sex is casual and about as
important as a Chinese lunch, violence is manly, hatred
is natural, America is Hitler Germany, you have to kill
to live (especially in the cities), and we're all headed
for extinction by either war or pollution or fornication
(read overpopulation) sometime between 1984 and
2001. So these movies haven't merely mirrored the
horrors of our time. They've helped to create them
and *legitimatize* them. So go, by all means, because
more values are being forged in that darkened theater
than in all our congressional halls, churches and
homes laid together (which will probably be the theme
of Kubrick's next picture).

The generation gap spreads its tentacles right
through the movie audience. While the demented
masked youths on screen beat the bejesus out of the
helpless husband, then rape his wife to the accompani-
ment of lively music and an insouciant little jig to keep
up the gaiety, the audience reactions break down by
age. The young are mostly numb for, after all, isn't the
screen just bringing My Lai and muggings and Watergate and assassinations home to us oldsters (who pre-
sumably were not aware of these obscenities before),
some of them giggling softly at the sheer spine-tingling
audacity of it all, a few even identifying themselves
with the daring devils on the screen. The genuine oldsters in the audience begin to wonder what the hell

they are doing there (they *forgot* that their sweet little granddaughter pushed them in by telling them it was "fantastic") and escape into the sunlight as if out of a snakepit. But you, you are pinned to your seat by your own ambivalences, like a fly to flypaper, and the producers have you where they want you. Your stomach gets queasy, you gag slightly, you throw sidelong glances at your reeling mate. You want to get up and flee, but something inside you says no, you have to *understand.* Maybe they're right. You have to suffer. You have to pay your dues, which are a hell of a lot higher than the price of admission. You, too, must learn to enjoy (or at least endure) the New Pornography, which is not the stag film at the Rotarians but the much-heralded youth films of our time (hailed by the august critics) that romanticize bloodshed and violence, turn sex into an empty sensation, reduce human relations to the jungle of claws and fangs and make the future an apocalypse of despair and doom. One of the virtues of the New Pornography is that, like a bad toothache, ordinary life seems so much better afterward. So go, but not on an empty stomach!

THE THEATER

For relief, and because you are bright and sophisticated and came across some "twofers" (two tickets for the price of one . . . the play is dying), you must go to the theater. If you live in or around New York City, Broadway beckons. Off Broadway is even better. You're more likely to get mugged down in the Village than on the Great White Way, but not much more. In either event, parking is a wondrous ordeal. You will probably not find a place to leave your car on the street and, if

by some chance you do, your car will be towed away
by the New York Police Department which is helpless
at fighting crime but so efficient at towing away cars
that one suspects the operation has been subcontracted
to the Mafia.

Whether Off Broadway or Broadway, however, the
substance of what appears on the boards will be the
same and, like the youth movie, it will be good for you.
It will be a racial theme and the point of it will be to
demonstrate, through free-flowing bloodshed and es-
calating traumas, what bastards we are! The players
may wear masks, and they are likely to spend much
time running through the audience with samurai
swords, but their message is clear: The *black man has*
been castrated and degraded by *you!* The theater's
answer to white racism is black racism, and it rectifies
the crime of stereotyping blacks by stereotyping whites.
In the modern dispensation, racial integration is a dis-
credited game played by white liberals (who are worse
than bigots because they live in Scarsdale) and black
identity is *up* while white ethnic identity (Italian,
Slovak, Polish) is tribal and a bummer. It is good for
you to participate in this modern exorcism of the dybbuk because, after all, it's your flabby dybbuk that
needs exercising and you can have the rare opportunity
to sweat guilt from every pore.

The delicious punishment is not limited to white
viewers either. The only blacks who can afford to throw
their money away on theater are middle class, and if
whitey gets his lumps in the racial theater, that's hom-
iny grits compared to what is visited upon the black
bourgeoisie. If you can afford to buy tickets to this
crummy show, you must have some bread. If you have
bread, you're part of the system. If you're part of the

system, you probably live in Grosse Pointe and turn your back on your brother! If you are upwardly mobile, you probably give to the NAACP, go to integrated cocktail parties and wish you were white. Comes the revolution, you'll get yours somewhere between the white liberal and the assimilated black who still calls himself Negro and is married to a nice zoftig Jewish girl from the Bronx.

If you have not yet received your due punishment in the theater, please hurry. The black thing is passing; the Jewish already gone; Indians, homosexuals, women and Formosan Chinese are jostling each other enroute to center stage. If you are alive and curious enough to ask yourself, who am I, then go to the theater, which has opened itself to the profound questions of life and of being. When you get the answer, there will be plenty of time later for you to slash your wrists.

THE STADIUM

There's nothing to compare with the electricity generated by a crowd at Madison Square Garden or Shea Stadium, or Chavez Ravine or any good sports palace in the country. Compared to this, watching a game on television is like taking a bath in your underwear. You have to *be* there, become part of the mass emotion, lose yourself in the crowd. This is truly a transforming entertainment. You spend your life, like a bureaucratic mole, sitting invisibly behind a desk in your office. Meek and conscientious, you have long since become part of the furniture of the place. "Sweet old dictator," the secretaries call you. But at the STADIUM you are a different person. You are a *tiger*. With a container of beer clutched in each paw, you are the first to leap to

your feet bellowing: *"Kill the bum! Throw the sonofabitch out! Hey, Sparky, shove it down his throat!
Stick it in his ear!"*

All the frustrations of your life become sublimated
at the park. You are not a pale bureaucrat any longer.
You are a hot-eyed Roman in the ancient Coliseum,
shrieking for blood. You are an African savage howling
for tribal warfare. You are a primitive child joining
your childish temper tantrum to the amplitude of thousands. In wild fantasy, *you* are the beautiful athlete
smashing the ball into the upper deck; *you* are the
dauntless relief pitcher, strutting to the mound; *you*
are the fleet-footed split end, streaking past the sec-
ondary; *you* are the sleek giant stuffing the basketball
through the hoop as the fans explode at the final buz-
zer. Technically you are a fan, but in reality you are
one of the key players, playing out your inner dreams,
acting out your deepest fantasies, rippling the muscles
of your buried imagination. Which is the real *you*—
the zombie at the office or the tiger in the tank?

THE OPERA

There are three ways to get to the opera. The first is
practice. The second, pursued by a friend of mine, is
to hire yourself out as an extra for small non-singing
parts. My friend was one of the footmen in *Aïda,* and
his job was to walk behind the horses in the famous
"Celeste Aïda" scene. Unfortunately, he choked in front
of the large audience, tripped and fell face down into
the horse's leavings. The third (better) is to pay your
money and go in and sit down like a mensh.

The standard operas are pips. What's not to delight
you with *Rigoletto, La Traviata, La Bohème* and the

like? Wagner is the sticking point. It separates the men
from the boys. You can avoid the dilemma by declar-
ing, a priori, that Wagner was an anti-Semite or a
precursor of the Nazis, thus copping out of the neces-
sity to subject yourself to him. But the gutsy way is to
go all out by attending *Die Meistersinger, Tristan und
Isolde* or *Das Rheingold. Die Meistersinger* runs on for
four and a half hours at the Metropolitan Opera. The
true aficionados have learned to sleep with their eyes
wide open, thus stirring no disapproval from the all-
out Wagner fans. If you doze off, be careful not to
snore because the Wagner fans are fanatics and you
could be stoned. Also, after sleeping through the entire
act, be sure to awaken at the curtain and prove you are
alive by hurling bravos at the singers and beating your
hands together until they are pulp. Also, remember
to wear hip pads to guard against your wife who will
keep trying to elbow you awake, all the while hissing:
"At these prices, the least you can do is keep your eyes
open!"

Opera is a tonic for middle-aged people. It lifts a
curtain on a world of color, drama, lilting beauty and
opulent make-believe. And even if the mezzo soprano
looks like a Mack truck and moves about the stage with
the agility of Dick Butkus, even if it takes her twenty-
two minutes on the clock to expire after being stabbed
by an avenging baritone, even if those people in the
middle of your row always arrive late and walk on your
shoes, even if your wife has perforated your rib cage
with her elbow—despite everything, opera is an exhila-
rating experience, especially if you remember to smug-
gle a tiny transistor radio in your pocket to listen to
the baseball game.

WALKING

One of the best forms of entertainment and recreating
is just walking. Why continue to take the car two
blocks to the neighborhood drugstore or around the
corner for bagels? You should be ashamed. If riding
the bicycle is too strenuous for you, then learn to walk.
It is not difficult.

Just place your best foot forward, propel your body
ahead, then put out your other foot and, before you
know it, you will be moving forward under your own
power. It is like swimming; soon you will not even be
conscious of the movements, it will be automatic. Once
you have learned to walk, where should you go?

You can visit neighbors, watch the birds, picket, buy
a newspaper or return the Book of the Month selection
you don't want. It doesn't matter; the crucial thing is
to start your motor and get yourself moving. Walking
is good exercise and it is also good entertainment. It
clears the mind and quickens the spirit. It also gets
you out into the unacceptable air, but this is a small
price for getting out of the house to become part of the
passing world. On a good day, you can stop at the park
and sit on a bench and read the paper, lick a popsickle
or munch a salami sandwich or feed the pigeons.

All you need to become a good walker is Italian
boots, pink Bermudas and a maroon sweatshirt saying
"Property of French Lick, Michigan." If you live in the
suburbs, walking around will make you suspect, and
the local gendarmes may follow and hassle you a bit,
but all you need to do is to show them a receipt for
your local property tax bill and they'll lay off. The
neighbors will put you down as a loony and the motor-

cycle kids may try to run you down, but walk on, walk on with your head held high, and leave ill enough alone!

PEOPLE

But, after all is said and done, the best entertainment is still PEOPLE . . . alive, irascible, wondrous. Become a *people* person—and enjoy your middle age. People are falsely divided by race, religion, money and age. But there is only one *valid* division: the *up* people and the *down* people. Wherever possible, stay with the *uppers* and avoid, like the plague, the *downers*. (If you live in New York City, move to San Francisco.) The *uppers* have a zest and a gaiety for life; they like to laugh and sing; they give people the benefit of the doubt, and they tend to look on the brighter side of things. They will lend you money without interest. The *downers* go around looking grim, mumbling, "Shit, there's nothing to do" and/or "This ain't my day." Their conversation usually consists of dropping a load of their troubles on the nearest victim (you) while looking at you balefully, as if you were about to molest them, if you should be foolish enough to discuss *your* problems with *them*. They have no interest in lending you money. You may not be able to control your choices, because *downers* attract other *downers* while *uppers* seem simply to skip and glide to other *uppers*. To help you to at least identify the type, insert *U* or *D* (or *T* for Trick Question) after each of the following statements.

1. I don't believe that goddam mechanic even opened the hood before he made out this whopping bill.—

2. The World Series is fixed.—

3. How am I? Aside from rectal bleeding, neuras-
thenic anxiety, incipient hernia, melancholic depression
and beri beri, I'm terrible.—

4. I'm an optimist. I think things today are lousy.—

5. The only honest politician is a dead one.—

6. Life is very much worth living, if you call this
living.—

7. I am one of the few people who likes me.—

8. Contrary to what everyone else says, I think you're
okay.—

9. The reason I do all the talking is that I like good
conversation.—

10. I love humanity but hate people.—

11. I fight poverty—I *work!*—

12. I thanked a green plant today.—

VIII

Politics

Middle age is, for some reason, a time for growing
conservatism—the browning of America. While your
children are getting ready to tear up the system by the
short hairs, you are becoming increasingly wedded to
the status quo (which is defined as "the mess we are
in"). The wild and passionate visions of your own
flaming youth begin to cool like newly mixed jello in
the refrigerator. Only you don't like to admit it. You
don't call it conservatism. (You prefer to say a liberal
is somebody who has not yet been mugged.) You call
it wisdom, experience, judgment, conserving the best
of the past. It is not easy to abandon the ideals of your
youth—particularly since your own youngsters are now
committed to those same ideals—so you need a set of
graceful "outs" to justify your retreat. Here are some of
the best:

1. "LA PLUS ÇA CHANGE, LA PLUS C'EST LA MEME
CHOSE." This is French, which makes it impressive. It
must be recited, despite your pidgin French, in a tone
of jaded philosophic resignation. Translated into English, it comes down to: Why bother to change things

anyway? When used on your children, it entitles you to a lengthy monologue on the many times in the past that this particular idea has been trotted out and how, inevitably, it has fallen on its face. This is especially good in connection with women's lib ("So tell me, women's suffrage improved the world?") and sexual freedom, because it permits you to get in a lick about the Romans and Greeks and how all that sleeping around, he-ing and she-ing and he-ing and he-ing led to decadence and collapsing empires.

2. "LISTEN, ROME WASN'T BURNED IN A DAY!" This is a blockbuster of an out. After all, *can* you change things overnight? Invocation of this eternal wisdom is most effective when someone is trying to get rid of war, discrimination, sickness and overpopulation through the passage of legislation. This should be said solemnly as if it were holy writ hot from Sinai.

3. "WAIT UNTIL YOU HAVE TO MEET A PAYROLL." This should wipe out your starry-eyed young. It puts them right in their place. How can they know the solutions to social problems if they have never met a payroll? Thus, you should be able to stifle idle chatter about redistribution of income, a national health plan, guaranteed annual wages or any other half-baked notions. If business experience alone can certify one's opinions on such matters, what do your kids know, considering they are, respectively, a carpenter's helper, a potter, a hawker of peace bands and a VISTA worker?

4. "MAN DOES NOT LIVE BY BREAD ALONE." This is very effective when the issue is that some deprived group wants its share of bread. How better to put down the blacks without being called racist? How better to dismiss the migrant workers without being called selfish? You're not a bigot. Voila! You're *spiritual*. There is

something ineffable that transcends such trivia as human rights, welfare and minimum wage. It is *spiritual* and since that is beyond you and everyone else, you don't have to lift a finger in the here and now, which is just as well because you're going bowling tonight anyway while your kids will sit with their guru, plumb their souls, read poetry and recite their ooms.

5. "LISTEN, THERE'S MORE TO LIFE THAN HAPPINESS." This is the equivalent of "Life is not a bowl of cherries." You spring this "out" when, for example, your daughter says she's not *happy* at college, your son says he's not *happy* living in the city and/or your wife says she's not *happy* doing housework all day. You sound very convincing in this out until they ask you: "Like what?" Or "Name three!" The truth is that you use this out only when somebody *else's* pursuit of his constitutional right to happiness impinges on yours. . . .

One of the best things you can do to keep yourself alive and vigorous is to plunge into politics. It is a hair-raising experience and, by the looks of your thinning locks, you could use it. Now that you have made the commitment to plunge, what should it be? As a candidate for Congress, as a volunteer (holding someone else's coat) or as an armchair kibbitzer? Let us examine the alternatives.

CANDIDATE

The first requirement for a candidate for Congress is money. Politics in America is a rich man's game. It takes a minimum of seventy-five thousand dollars to run for Congress and a lot more if you have a primary fight. You do not have to be personally rich (any more than you have to be crazy), but it helps. If you don't have money yourself, you had better have lots of friends who are loaded. Of course, you will be obligated to them and to their special interests (whom do you know at ITT or AT&T?) after you are elected, but that's better than losing, isn't it? Since it is already obvious that you do not meet this first requirement, let's move rapidly to the second.

The second requirement is charisma. Nobody can describe just what that quality is—a blend of sex appeal, *shmaltz* and electricity—but, whatever it is, you have no more of this than you had of the previous requirement. Charisma cannot be manufactured or counterfeited. Either you've got it or you haven't. The opposite of charisma is mackerel, which just lies there. You are a very nice person, but you couldn't draw a crowd in the subway during rush hour.

The third requirement is to be a lawyer. This is not a constitutional or legal requirement, just one sanctified by practice. It stems from the need to have big mouths in Congress. One look at the United States Congress, larded with large-bottomed lawyers capable of a filibuster at the drop of a hat, gives the public a needed reassurance that the lawmakers will do nothing hasty— indeed will do nothing, period. (Calling a lawyer's product a "brief" is one of the great misnomers of our time.) The lawyer is also specially qualified to steer business to his law firm and, when he runs to seed so visibly as to be an embarrassment, can always be made a judge, thus preserving the continuity of our system. But, as a non-lawyer, you don't answer this requirement either.

Fourth—and least important—is: What do you *stand* for? This is least important inasmuch as you have already flunked out on the prior three and, also, because nobody really cares about what a candidate for Congress stands for. The public wasn't fazed by the candidate in Ohio who, when asked about Formosa, said he would carry it by thirty thousand votes. Or by the candidate who, when asked if his wife was a thespian, threatened to sue. You can always run against "busing," "crime," "welfare chiselers" and "eggheads" and in favor of the "American Way of Life." The weightier question is: What does the *public* stand for? And the dismal answer is: Practically everything. We, the public, stand for doddering old fools and young plastic clowns who run the government like a private fief, truancy, corruption, ignorance, bigotry, deception, demagoguery, seniority and filibuster rules which mangle the democratic process, and elected officials who haven't told the truth in more than fifty years. So, it is clear, you don't qualify as a candidate for Congress.

So, run for President. The only qualification to run for this office is that you be thirty-five years of age and a native of the United States. Beyond that, no qualifications whatsoever are required, as you can see from having lived through several recent Presidents. Any country that can survive our recent Presidents can't be all bad. Until we move toward the truly democratic process of drawing the President out of a hat or winning him in a lottery instead of selling the office to the highest bidders, there is no conceivable reason why you should not run for it. Everyone else does, including Pat Paulsen, Sam Yorty and other comedians. All that is required is a modicum of chutzpah, some money, a strong dose of egomania, a saving grace of paranoia (just because you *fear* that people are trying to destroy you doesn't mean that they are *NOT*) and an advertising agency which can stretch your minor strengths so that they can fill out a thirty-second subliminal TV spot.

If you are a member of a minority group—black, Chicano, Jewish, women, Indian and/or gay—you will have a head start in your race. Some candidates in 1972 had understandable doubts that a black man could be elected Veep in the present climate. They may have been right, but with the astounding success of Golda Meir in Israel, Indira Gandhi in India and Shirley Chisholm and Bella Abzug in Congress, the timing may be ripe for a *black Jewish woman* in the White House. The prospect boggles the imagination. It gives one to think . . .

HOW THE UNITED STATES GOT ITS
FIRST BLACK JEWISH WOMAN PRESIDENT*

The incredible events of 1984 were too bizarre to be believed, but they happened. The Democratic National Convention took place in the recently completed Dome in New Orleans. It was the first convention with instant replay television fiddling on the roof. It was the first convention where the riots, confined mostly to the French Quarter, were witnessed by the delegates and the watching world at the same moment. The rioters were women libbers, gay libbers, Indians, Jewish Defense Leaguers, Italian and Polish ethnics, Chicanos and—a newly emergent political force—the MAD DOGS (Middle-aged Deprived, Disgusted Over Governmental Short-changing) whose fierce mock barking (and urinating on the trees) filled Bourbon Street and scared the bejesus out of senior citizens (organ-

* A revised version of "A Jew in the White House," which first appeared in *American Judaism* in the spring of 1961.

ized under the banner of Gray Panthers) and wine-
stoned youth left over from the Mardi Gras.

The convention moguls were terrified. It was 1968 all
over again, and violence in the streets would once more
wreck the party and, if they proceeded as planned, to
nominate Hubert Humphrey again would surely lose
them the election to David Eisenhower who had risen
to fame as chairman of the Committee to Free the Watergate 500. What to do? It was a moment of crisis, a
time for radical improvisation. How to cool the riots,
how bind up this strange new motley coalition of fury
on the twisted streets of New Orleans? It was Julian
Bond (no longer youthful nor black) who popped the
audacious idea: Stella Argash! She had it all—female
(Joan of Arc to women), the very archetype of Middle
Age, black and Jewish (and, therefore, a sop to all
the white ethnics, even including the JDLers who
hated her guts), darling of the gay liberationists (she
had been the first politician to campaign by cruising in
gay bars), with a summer home in Cuernavaca, Mexico
(where she later established one of her vacation White
Houses along with a black White House in Nairobi,
a floating Italian White House on a vaporetto in Venice,
an Indian teepee on 75th Street in Manhattan and a
pagoda called Taka Metziah in Tokyo). And, with
three hot shvitz baths a day, the cleanest politician in
the land.

It was a stroke of pure genius. The delegates
swallowed hard, gulped, gagged and bit the bullet.
Stella became the Democratic candidate for President
of the USA. . . .

As history so radiantly records, Stella was elected in
a landslide. She carried every state—including Euphoria
—and blitzed the ethnic, urban, minority, woman and

middle-aged vote. Forswearing jets and TV, she *walked*
from coast to coast with a shopping bag, shmoosing
with the voters. The only substantial opposition was
a group of Jewish leaders who ambushed her on the
road from Forest Park in St. Louis, and begged her
a week before the election to withdraw from the race,
arguing that election of a black Jew would foment
anti-Semitism (which they described as disliking Jews
more than absolutely necessary) and racism and that
she would not be able to give Phantoms to Israel as
Nixon did or put a black on the Supreme Court as
Johnson did. Shirley Chisholm also denounced her as
an Auntie Tam. Stella told them where to put their
protests and went on, unflappable, to a mammoth and
resounding victory.

She was an extraordinary President, putting all of
her diverse backgrounds to work for the country. She
eliminated the value-added sales tax and replaced it
with a hard-sell UJA-type campaign for the USA which
doubled national income in a year. Everyone became
a Big Giver, a Man of the Year and a Champion of
Liberty. She called for a Marshall Plan to rebuild the
cities and financed it by pressuring every American to
make a once-in-a-lifetime pledge, payable in ten years,
as a life member of the USA; at the end of five years,
even New York City was inhabitable again and the
country joined in a televised mortgage-burning cere-
mony from the White House (which she personally
scoured with Mr. Clean to disinfect Watergate smells).
She got rid of the busing issue by organizing car pools
in every city. She had a pushka (a red, white and blue
can) placed in every American home with a formula
for payment for cuss words, fibs and other trespasses.
She legalized numbers as well as pot and had it sold

instead of cigarettes in vending machines with all proceeds put in the revenue-sharing pot. Like the skilled
housewife she was, she cut so much fat out of the
defense budget that it was leaner, tastier and digestible
(like a veal cutlet) for the first time in thirty years.

And she reordered national priorities to put health,
education, jobs, mass transit and housing first. The
Cabinet was weird but effective. It consisted of an
ac/dc Chicano, a lesbian, Martha Mitchell, an Indian,
an Italian grandmother, a leader of the MAD DOGS
and a Chasidic Jew who taught the Cabinet to eat
soul food kosher style, to sing and dance with ecstasy
and to give the whole country a model of unity through
diversity. She brought the country together again and
she even stopped the persistent campaign led by Am-
bassador Archie Bunker, General Thieu and John
Connally to make South Vietnam the fifty-first state.

But Stella had her problems, of course. She was too
much the Jewish Mother. The Jewish lust for education
became a national obsession. Mothers began to register
their children at fancy private schools at the moment
of their birth. Competition became so fierce that some
mothers telephoned the schools at the moment of con-
ception and school switchboards lighted up in the
middle of the night (once, during a power failure, the
switchboard exploded). Unlike the old days when
mothers would greet poor grades of their children by
saying: "I'll kill you!" American mothers, deeply in-
fluenced by the Jewish Mother in the White House,
now cried: "I'll kill myself!" It turned the country
around. Stella's slogan was: "Don't burn your bras—
don't burn the cities—burn the midnight oil, baby!"
Black mothers organized to educate their children with
all the fury of Jewish mothers.

The other problem was, of course, in foreign policy
—predictably the Middle East. It happened early in
her term . . . 1985, as a matter of fact . . . when
Egypt breached the Nile River cease-fire and invaded
Israel, thus touching off the Six Hour War. To the
consternation of the world, the new cease-fire found
Israel occupying the capitals of Amman, Damascus,
Cairo and—incredibly—Moscow. It took all of Stella's
persuasive power, along with our only ally in the world
—Red China—to persuade the Israeli prime minister,
Shoshanna Herzog, *not* to proclaim the Greater Israel
and also to withdraw the Israeli commander from
Moscow. "If you don't get the hell out of there, I'll
put out your other eye," she allegedly said to Moshe
Dvir. It worked. "We Jews shouldn't wash our dirty
linen in public," Dvir said from Moscow.

Except for these minor pogroms, her presidency
was a triumph. Women's rights were exalted. Civil
rights were consummated and protected. Racism and
anti-Semitism became confused and diluted. Abortions
and vasectomies were provided free upon demand
through the national health service. The Constitution,
the Congress, and the courts were resurrected. Every
municipality which cleaned up its air and water got
the U-kosher seal and any American who quit smoking
and/or driving a car got a plaque on both his houses.
America was not just one society again; it was a vast,
multihued and diverse mishpocheh presided over by
a black Jewish mother who drove both Le Roi Jones
and Philip Roth right up the wall. . . .

Stella spoke to the American people on national
television once a week—the "Fireside Shmoos" was
jointly sponsored by Vita Herring, Manischewitz Wine,
Kentucky Fried Chicken and Alka-Seltzer (whose stock

split in the boom brought on by the zooming national popularity of Jewish and soul cooking). She refused to be made up and talked to the nation ("So, listen, sisters and brothers . . .") with her afro in curlers. Each week she read a letter from a citizen and responded on the air. One was from Stella's mother-in-law, complaining that she wouldn't eat in the White House until Stella brought in separate dishes, put a *mezuzah* on the door and moved the White House to the suburbs. Another was from a Jewish lady, brokenhearted that her daughter was emigrating to Israel: "After all I have done for *Hadassah!*" Still another was from a black mother who wrote: "I have prayed that blacks and Jews would be reconciled again, but I never dreamed it would be in the person of the *President*, in the *White* House yet! Such a nice mishegass! Right on, Sister Stella!"

Stella left office in high honor in 1992 and was succeeded by her disciple, Dollar Bill Bradley of the New York Knicks, apostle of the last remaining, forgotten and abused minority, the WASPs of America.

IX

Religion: Try It; You'll Like It

So you would like to give some time to community and humanitarian concerns? It's about time. You have been a member of your church (or temple) for years, but you have used it primarily as a service station (religious school, confirmation, rites of passage and a place to park the kids). Now is the time to do more than pay your dues and use the place for your own purposes. Now, in your middle years, is the time to get involved, personally and deeply.

WHY RELIGION?

But why go to religion? Why not to the Lions or Rotarians or the local civic association?

There are many good reasons for doing this. One is that young people are abandoning the local church and temple in droves, so there is one place you can go without having a bunch of raunchy kids underfoot. Another reason is that you're getting to the age where you should be hedging your bet anyway. If there IS a God, He'll be impressed. If there is NOT, there is certainly a clergyman (albeit a lesser deity to worship) who will be equally impressed by the availability of another warm body in the congregation.

But the most important reason you should go is that the religious institution is a reminder of the sanctity of the human personality, regardless of race, sex, religion or age. It is a monument to the dignity of man. It provides spiritual satisfaction by placing before you the eternal goals of life. It makes you realize there is something bigger in life than yourself—and that is the local clergyman with the limp wrist (from laying on of hands), the interfaith smile and the Mount Rushmore face. You should be a part of the great mysteries of life, one of which is how *that* congregation is going to pay off its two-million-dollar mortgage.

In addition, it is a groovy emotional outlet. During the months leading up to the decision on whether or not to renew the clergyman's contract, you will enjoy an emotional excitement which combines all the lovely primitive attributes of a political campaign, a pogrom, a Ku Klux Klan revival meeting and the ancient Christians being fed to the lions. Raising your faltering voice in the communal singing of hymns is good for the soul, but it is small potatoes compared to the ecstasy of plunging your full being into the local jihad (holy war) between the guerrillas and the loyalists in the contract renewal struggle. This is known in contemporary church parlance as *total commitment* and it is a gas, especially when the young clergyman comes in fired with enthusiasm—and leaves the same way.

There's a new wrinkle in the process of hiring the clergyman. A congregation in Michigan has announced that it will only engage a spiritual leader after "favor-

able results from professional psychological testing."
Leaving aside the question of whether the members
of the Pulpit Committee should not themselves be put
through the psychological wringer, one can only imagine how the psychological once-over will work. . . .

Once the clergyman's wife has been examined, and
the applicant himself is horizontal on the couch, how
about these free-association questions to the aspiring
clergyman for openers?

1. How do you react when the president of the congregation says to you: "Maybe you didn't learn this in
the seminary, but we've got to have your leadership
in raising funds for the new building. Can you learn
how to buttonhole every member, turn him upside
down and shake out all his money?"

2. What do you say when the president of the
Sisterhood exults after your sermon: "You live by the
sweat of your tongue!"

3. What response do you make when, in the wake
of your fiery sermon on the plight of the migrant
workers, one of your Board members says: "So, tell
me, what's Jewish (or Christian) about LETTUCE?"

4. What words of wisdom do you have for the
married man who comes to you for counseling and
complains: "I just read *The Sensuous Woman* and
my wife flunks every chapter."

5. How do you answer (and why) when, after you
have painted the horrors of the Burundi holocaust,
one of your sprightlier senior citizens seizes your hand
and exults: "I just LOVED your sermon!"

6. What is your very first impulse when you drive
to services and find that someone has violated your
Eleventh Commandment, "Thou shalt not park in the
clergyman's parking space."

7. What do you say when you give a powerful lesson on racial justice and one of the big givers to the building fund says: "So tell me, sir, if you like them so much, why don't you live in Harlem?" (This is the same big giver who dramatically announced he was *doubling* his building pledge. On checking, it turns out he had given *nothing* before.)

8. What is the first thing that comes to your mind when a committee of the Board waits upon you to discuss your wife's décolletage and miniskirts?

9. How do you feel when you decide that you need one morning a week just to *think*, without interruption by telephone or visitors, and it evokes a storm of angry disapproval from the members ("We hired him, and he's got to be available when we need him")? Suggestion: If, instead of saying you are busy "thinking," your secretary says you are "studying," everything will come up roses!

10. How do you react when you first see the parsonage (which is a rabbit's warren behind the sanctuary) and your wife informs you that she would rather establish residence in the local abattoir?

HEART ATTACKS, RELEVANCE AND INNOVATION

Religion is also very healthy, believe it or not—not only emotionally, but physically. Israel recently completed its Ischemic Heart Disease Project, one of the largest such studies in the world. The project analyzed various environmental factors, suggesting which ways of life reduce the incidence of heart attack. The researchers asked: Do you go to the synagogue daily, sometimes or rarely? Those who prayed daily had the lowest incidence of heart attacks (twenty-nine per a

thousand persons), "sometimes" next (thirty-seven per
a thousand) and "rarely" the most (fifty-six out of a
thousand). Turns out the daily worshiper tended to
smoke less, to lead a more regular life. Also significant
was exercise (the least the worst) and a loving wife
(the more the better). The lesson is obvious: If you
want to avoid heart attacks, try religion and go whole
hog—become an Orthodox Jew working as a carpenter
in the Galilee who doesn't smoke and who has a wife
who loves him (a great deal, but not to death), and
who is chairman of the Pulpit Committee (he *gives*
heart attacks, doesn't *have* them!).

You will also want to get in on the RELEVANCE
bit which is (or *was*, it may be out of date) sweeping
American religious institutions. The idea here is,
plainly, to get *with* it. The point to *relevance* is to
deal with the truly important issues in contemporary
society and not to hide the light of your faith under
the bushel basket of the institution. For Catholics, this
means fighting dirty movies; for Protestants, getting
Christmas onto postage stamps; and for Jews, knocking
Christmas off postage stamps. *Relevance* is very important, particularly in our day when nobody cares
much about lesser issues like repentance, faith, belief,
sin, communion, prayer, charity, education and other
equally obsolete matters on which religion has so long
been hung up.

(Some deep religious thinkers are suggesting that
relevance should not be connected to the question of
SPEAKING OUT. They point out that lately the churches
have been *speaking out* on the great issues of war and
peace and slums and ecology, but these things seem
only to have gotten worse as a result. Dr. Reinhalt
Nebber has said: "The main trouble with the churches'

speaking out is that they really have nothing to *say.* In the past, we have condemned the churches for silence. Nowadays we should condemn them for *noise pollution.* What the churches should do now is to make a virtue of silence. If they could get hold of clean air and pump it into their sanctuaries and let Quaker silence be the entire service, they would soon be mobbed with people looking for a place to breathe, meditate and enjoy a sanctuary of silence.")

Innovation is also big in religion today. The old traditions are all suspect; if it was done before, it is already passé. Renewal is the law of life and the winds of change blow through our sanctuaries with gale force, leveling the Latin liturgy, the old prayer books and the ancient forms. If the church or synagogue wants to be where it's at, it must be with it in the shopping plaza and the condominium. Religion is show biz.

Innovation means that you should not be surprised to see the service begin with the clergyman chanting a Chasidic nigun while descending from the rafters in a helium balloon as the choir bellows the hymn "Nearer My God to Thee." This may be followed by five males in loincloths, their bodies painted red with quotations from Richard Nixon quoting Chairman Mao, representing the Gay (Cocken) Liberation Front, while four female gurus strum guitars and recite their ooms and a marching band of black militants interrupts the service to demand fifty million dollars in reparations, two dollars down.

Revolutionizing the physical setting is also important. The battle cry of the Revolution is: *Unscrew the Pew!* Down with permanent seats. Up with improvisation—services in the round, the square service (for

traditionalists), small circles, tic-tac-toe formats, sim-
ulated pogroms, horizontal positioning, or a series of
walls for the parents to get up against in the family
service.

This type of innovation is very dramatic and provoc-
ative. It has brought both good news and bad news
to our congregations. The good news is that with a
Cecil B. De Mille cast of thousands on the altar we are
sure to have TV and the press covering. The bad news
is that innovation is intended to bring in the young
and the alienated—and doesn't. The young are too *religious* to be caught dead in a house of worship. And
the alienated always say: "I never go, but if I did go,
I would want it to be traditional." So innovation blows
through the sanctuary but the congregation inherits
the wind.

But what can you *do* as a member of a church or
temple? After all, God only knows you do not have a
religious background, a good religious education or
any special skills in congregational life. Good. Those
are precisely the criteria for a good committee member. You can volunteer for the Worship Committee,
the Pulpit Committee, the Education Committee, the
Ritual Committee, the Youth Committee and the Building Committee. This is called "Rising through the
Chairs." If you sit quietly, saying nothing, the members
of the committee will be eternally grateful because
one more ear banger they can do without. If you keep
attending regularly, they will certainly make you secretary of the committee (especially if you are a woman)
which, while it is not like being elected to the Hall
of Fame, is some kind of honor nonetheless. Do not
make any suggestion—they will only make you chairman of the committee.

Should it be necessary to say a few words, the following terms are highly recommended and de rigeur in swinging churchy settings: input, scenario, new ball game, witness, fellowship. If it's a temple, replace "witness" with "tachlis" and "fellowship" with "sisterhood." A few Latin expressions are the ladder to upward mobility in the religious organizational life: seriatum, ad hoc, de novo, sui generis, pro bono, caveat emptor, e pluribus unum and gornisht helfen are de rigueur among the modern worshipers of Baal. And Robert's Rules of Order will take you a lot further than Holy Scriptures.

AND LAST BUT NOT LEAST, THE REFRESHMENTS

If you still have spare time to give to the congregation, you can also become one of the bodies to listen to all the speakers who parade through the congregation each week. Some people go for spiritual refreshment and to have a pleasant nap, awakening just in time to ask the first question. One elderly lady in Philadelphia goes to every session for the refreshments. She comes wearing white tennis shoes and bearing a large brown paper bag and, while the speaker is haranguing the congregation, glides softly to the table where the collation is set up and dumps a quantity of pastries into her bag. She got into trouble only once when she hit the local synagogue (she finds refreshments in the temples so superior to the churches she is thinking of *converting*) and the weight of the absconded bagels broke through the bag, exploding on the floor like a bunch of hand grenades and bringing Harry Golden on the podium to a screeching halt. Only in America. Nobody wants to hurt her feelings, but if this lady

isn't stopped, it is only a matter of time before she
backs up a truck and empties the social hall of every
refreshment in sight, Mayor Rizzo or no Mayor Rizzo.

You ought to hurry up and join if you are not already a member, because the church and temple are
not long for this world. In a classical case of presiding
over the liquidation of their own empire, religious
leaders are splitting the air with vehement denuncia-
tions of themselves. What right do we have to have such
magnificent buildings when so many people live in
poverty? Why should we be nailed to a given building
when we live in such a mobile age? Why listen to a
preacher painting hell and pointing to heaven in this
age of McLuhan communication? Why sit around and
worship when we could be out giving alms to the poor?
Why pray in a group when each of us can pray in the
woods? Since the automobile is the real god of our
people, and television is our inner life, why maintain
the old forms? All these challenges will undoubtedly
lead to a self-fulfilling prophecy and you can expect
that by the year 2000 the surviving remnants of Christians and Jews will belong to a Mod Ecumenical
Cassette-Drive-In Sanctuary which will be built in an
Iowa cornfield to allow for future growth and which
will be presided over by a Hare Krishna Jesus Freak
(who plans to make aliyah to Israel) with a one
lifetime contract.

X

Join the Movement

You are living in one of the most critical eras of American history. Profound cultural, social and political movements convulse the land. And you sit there worrying about your gray hairs and fatty hips! There is a beautiful parable that says that when Moses threw the staff into the Red Sea, the sea, contrary to the expected miracle, did NOT divide itself to leave a dry passage for the Hebrews. Not until the first person jumped *into* the sea did the promised miracle happen and the waves recede. So jump into a movement already!

Ah, but which? Well, you could try the civil rights movement, for what could be grander than the moral struggle to vindicate equal rights for all Americans? So you rush to your neighbor, Jacobin Van Pelt, that aristocratic white American who has devoted his entire life to the cause of black freedom. Van Pelt shows you to his study which is papered with old plaques and citations from civil rights organizations and the

National Conference of Christians and Jews. You tell
Van Pelt that you want to get in on his movement.
"Forget it," says Van Pelt, "the movement is shot since
they took it over."

"Who?" you ask. "Commies?"

"No," he answers. "Blacks."

"But don't you still believe in civil rights?" you ask.

"Sure," he sighs, "but nobody else does. I organized
a campaign for busing to achieve integration of the
schools and I was condemned by a hundred neighbors—seventy-five whites and twenty-five blacks whom
I moved into the neighborhood in the '60s, all of whom
now call me 'honkey' and plan to move to a separate
but equal all-black neighborhood."

"Heavens!" you exclaim.

"Then I called on the mayor," he went on, "to put
up some low-cost housing in the community to bring
some poor people into the neighborhood."

"Good idea," you purr. "What happened?"

"The mayor called me a Commie, a delegation of
ethnics from Forest Hills in New York came and
burned an effigy of John Lindsay on my lawn, a committee of black bourgeoisies took out a full-page ad
saying I was trying to wreck their property values,
and a leader of the Welfare Rightniks had a press
conference on my front stoop and said: 'What gives
this honkey WASP Van Pelt the idea we would live
next door to HIM?'"

"Well, I guess that's the temper of the times," you
say philosophically, wrapping your arms comfortingly
around Van Pelt's sagging shoulders.

"I gave them all I had," Van Pelt sobs. "And, in
the end, I feel rejected . . . castrated."

"'There, there," you say. "It's not as bad as all that.

Maybe it's time you moved onto some other movement."

"Yes, I've been thinking about that," Van Pelt cries.
"Do you know anybody at Gay Lib?"

THE YOUTH MOVEMENT

If the civil rights movement is dead—or, at least,
breathing hard—perhaps you can join the youth movement. The counterculture may be a royal pain in the
behind, but there are some things you should definitely
learn from them. One is their attitude toward work.
Forget the fact that they can afford this indulgence
only because we, their foolish parents, have worked
our tails off. Yet, how can we fault them for saying
that people should not be slaves to their jobs, that
making a life is more important than making a living,
that people should work to *live* but never live to *work*,
that worshiping the big buck is the worst form of
idolatry?

We can also learn from the counterculture that there
is something phony about our snob pecking order.
Why is a doctor higher on the social scale than a
basket weaver, a lawyer higher than a furniture maker,
a dentist higher than a toll collector? Because he
makes more money? Where is it written that should
be the criterion? No, the criteria should be: (1) the
work fosters personal growth and self-fulfillment; (2)
produces a person, product or service which is organ-
ically pure; (3) causes hurt to no consenting person.

From the counterculturists we can also learn that
nobody should stay in the same job more than five
years. Anyone who stays in one place long enough to
get a watch should be deemed guilty of a capital

crime. We have revered stability too long—who wants
to live in a stable? Now we should value change and
spontaneity. Every man or woman worth his (or her)
salt should have four or five different careers in a
lifetime. Stay out of ruts!

But changing your work is not as important as
changing your life style. Where your head is is more
important than where your bottom is. So why not move
to the woods of New Hampshire, the mountains of
New Mexico, the fjords of Norway, the shores of Lake
Galilee or the wilds of Kenya? To hell with punching
a clock and fighting traffic. Live close to the earth
under a clear sky and be your own man. That's
what we must learn from the youth culture.

To see just where the youth movement is at right
now, you take a trip to Berkeley to look up Carlo
Shmendrick, in the 1960s one of the holy terrors of
the college riots, notorious member of the California
Eleven and Maoist revolutionary. You find him in a
tower suite of the Hotel St. Francis in San Francisco,
manicuring his nails.

"Sakes alive, Mr. Shmendrick," you exclaim. "I would
never have recognized you."

"Oh, you mean the crew cut, the Bond Brothers
suit, the bow tie, the Phi Beta Kappa key chain and
all that? Well, the raunchy, smelly freak scene has
had it, didn't you know?"

"Heaven's sake, Shmendrick," you gasp. "Have you
sold out?"

"Oh, no, I didn't leave the counterculture. It left ME.
The young people are turned off on politics. They're
all on head trips. The drug scene has been contracted
to the Mafia. The communes are breaking apart in
internal squabbles. The peace movement has been de-

prived of Vietnam. And all those freaks have gone back to business school so they can take over their fathers' businesses and buy boats. The counterculture is as passé as an old McGovern-Eagleton button."

"I'm amazed," you sputter. "Then what do YOU do?"

"I work with my hands. I'm a plumber. In 1970 the government discovered that ordinary plumbers would no longer make house calls and so the government had to hire its own plumbers to fix leaks in the White House. I was hired."

"By the White House?"

"Yes, they gave me a wrench to fix leaks and a screwdriver to screw our enemies."

"But you had been an enemy yourself?"

"If you can't lick 'em, join 'em. On the side I'm secretary of the Committee to Secure Amnesty for the Watergate 500," he said, lighting up a Havana cigar. "I figure things won't get better until we coronate King Richard Nixon."

"But," you continue, sputtering, "a king is against the Constitution!"

"That's what the bug-out brigade says, but after we abolish the Congress, we plan to impound the Supreme Court and give the media the royal treatment!"

WHITEMAIL

Well, if there's no room for you in the civil rights movement or the youth movement, how about the peace movement? So you jump in the car and drive over to the college, long the bastion of the peace movement. You find a few long-haired kids, but they are stretched out on the lawn, taking in the sun. The movement is now a mere spasm, and the roaring lions have become pussycats. Most of the active students, you note, are brisk middle-aged types who are destroying the character of the college by confusing college with EDUCATION. They want credits, grades, degrees and they have no time for hanky-panky or causes. But, certainly, there must be some remnant of a peace movement left. You call upon the Protestant chaplain who spent years in jail for blowing up a draft board during the Vietnam war. Where is the peace movement? you ask him.

"The wake is over there," he waves languidly.

And there it was. Five students, clad only in peace chains, sitting in a friendship circle, lighting candles and mourning for the Vietnam war.

"If I forget thee, oh Vietnam war, let my right hand forget its cunning," intones one.

"Ah, Vietnam war, those were the best years of our lives," murmurs another. "We must not take Yes for a final answer."

"Without you, oh Vietnam war, life has lost its meaning, its purpose and its direction," sings another. "You are lost but not forgotten, dreadful sorry, Vietnam war."

"I knew that fascist bastard Nixon would take you from me, oh Vietnam war," mumbled another. "Leave us fast until the war resumes, for he has put the hearse before the cart."

"Come back, little Vietnam war, I cannot live without you," moans another. "You were the salvation and the light."

"The Vietnam war will rise again. Leave us keep

the faith. If we will it, resurrection is no dream. Only the holy Vietnam war can bring us back together again," they recited in chorused ooms, the last of the faithful mourning the death of their holy cause—like early gladiators in the Coliseum deprived of lions —and Jews.

Well, if the civil rights movement is gone and the youth culture has sold out, and the peace movement has burned out, what other movement is alive and well? There must be some place for you. So you check out the women's lib movement and—sure enough— there is enough surging vitality there to persuade you that the women's revolution, unlike many others which degenerate into faddism, is *here to stay*.

So you go to Houston to attend a gigantic convention of the women's lib movement and your heart pounds with excitement. Unfortunately, however, the libbers place you and the other men behind a rope at the back of the room, right under the amplifying system, and Bella Abzug (chairperson) blows out your right eardrum. You try to move your seat but a large usherette mau maus you in the back of the room while a dozen smiling feminists yell, "Right on!" You sit down and listen to a stormy debate about lesbianism among one leader who says, "a/c-d/c is an optional way of life," another who says it is a blessing, and a third who says it is a political force which must be reckoned with. Confused, you wander into a consciousness-raising session where twenty-two women are throwing poisoned darts at blown-up photographs of Norman Mailer, Richard Nixon and Midge Decter, while the Gay Cocken Liberation Front demonstrates in a closet outside the room and a cadre of transvestites throw

a coming-out party. You can't figure out which side
you are on, so you go home wondering.

THE ETHNIC MOVEMENT

Is there then no movement where you can get involved? Find yourself. Do not despair. The movement
that is a true sleeper today is the ETHNIC MOVE-
MENT. This is the only movement that is really on
the rise. The Chicanos, the Irish, the Greeks, the Italians, the Indians, the Chinese, the Jews (who can't
figure out whether they are a religion, a minority
group, a nationality, a race or an ethnic group) are
only the tip of the iceberg. All are feeling their oats,
deepening their identity, asserting their interests and
widening their consciousness. So, get cracking. Join
an *ethnic* movement and become a real *leader* in
American life.

If you attend five successive meetings of your local
civic association, church or temple auxiliary, service
association or political club, they will elect you president or chairman and you can have a brief ego trip,
which is good for the psyche. But these things are
Mickey Mouse activities indeed. This is no longer
where the action is. The red meat nowadays is to become an *ethnic leader.* If you are Laotian, Lithuanian,
Litvak, Hungarian, whatever—you have a golden opportunity. You see, we now know that the old American melting pot never worked. Instead of a melting
pot, it turned out to be a cross between a pressure
cooker and a cockpit. So, in this day of intense ethnic
consciousness, every group is in business for itself, ir-
ritated and jealous of every other group, and in search
of a charismatic leader to get its forces together.

How do you get to be a *leader?* In the first place, it has nothing to do with the democratic process—that's glacially slow and works poorly anyway. It has nothing to do with merit, which is an obsolete quality. It is done through television, which anoints the leaders in each ethnic group. Here is how it is done: You get in front of the camera, spit in its eye and threaten to burn City Hall down unless the "Establishment" immediately solves whatever grievances your ethnic group has nursed for a generation. By morning (or, earlier, right after the 11:00 P.M. news) you will be proclaimed by the media as the new ethnic *leader,* thus displacing the fellows who have devoted their entire lives to the laborious process of serving their communities. The mayor of your city will dispatch a committee of five to negotiate your non-negotiable demands with you. He will also fly in, by helicopter, a team of encounter psychologists who will lock you into a room with five other militant representatives of your aggrieved group to "play T-group games" with the mayor, chief of police and three other Establishment finks from the city leadership. Thereafter, all this having led to nothing, the mayor will co-opt you with a nice sinecure job in the poverty program (there's good money in poverty) in the very nick of time because, just before the six o'clock news, a neophyte and rival from your ethnic group will knock you out of the picture with a threat to turn on the entire city by flooding the reservoirs with LSD unless . . .

The ethnic groups are quite interchangeable. That's why the Jews, the Italians and the women all have anti-defamation leagues and their meetings, as you will see in a moment, are all the same . . .

RIGHT ON WITH THE ITALIANS—OR UP THE SO-CALLED
MAFIA*

The Italians are rebelling. The recent massive demonstration in New York City, protesting ethnic slurs
in the fight against the Mafia, indicated that Italians
are beginning to behave like other aggrieved minorities.
It also demonstrates that the melting pot is getting unstuck with a vengeance. There is nothing like a seeming
crisis to bring together diverse and conflicting elements
within the group. Judging from what happens within
the other ethnic establishments, one can only imagine
a behind-the-scenes emergency meeting for the purpose of knocking heads together so that all organizations could march in the rain under one *Italian* um-
brella. . . .

Joe Signato opened the meeting, saying: "Okay,
okay, so who called this meeting?"

Tony Carrizoni explained: "*Nobody* called this meeting. This is a *non-auspices* ad hoc meeting of *all*
Italian organizations. We know that if any *one* organization called it, the rest of us wouldn't show, right?"

"Right on," said Mrs. Alitio, fist clenched.

"Now, to proceed," proceeded Tony. "We are here
to respond to an emergency; we are sick of being
vilified by the FBI and by the media. We have had
enough of being identified with the goddam Mafia!"

"You mean the *so-called* goddam Mafia," put in
Mrs. Alitio. "There is no such thing! It is a myth, a
figment of the FBI's senile imagination."

"Right on," said Signato. "The damned papers are
up to their old tricks. The FBI picked up a paisano

* Adapted, with permission of *The Jewish Digest* (April 1971).

with a million-dollar load of narcotics in his violin case yesterday and, of course, his name was Fallachi so they automatically started up again about the Mafia. The time has come for us Italians to sit down and see where we stand!"

Mr. Muzzola said: "My organization doesn't see this as an Italian problem. It's an American problem. We say the Italian community cannot take responsibility for individual Italians who go astray. We're against any cockamamey public action. You don't speak for me."

Mr. Carrizoni raised his hand. "I hate to agree with Muzzola because he is almost always wrong," he said, "but how do we know the publicity is harmful? That's an assumption. Let's hire Gallup to see whether this publicity is really affecting the public image of the Italians. My guess is that most Americans couldn't even tell you who Fallachi is, much less what his nationality is. Only Italians will know. We worry a lot."

"Ridiculous!" put in Mr. Delmonica. "You're kidding yourself. The publicity is terrible. *The Godfather* is the biggest thing since Creation. All those Italian words, the *Times* looks like the *Osservatore Romano*. I make my Bonito carry his violin in a suitcase; I should let him on the street with a violin case? I say we should issue a public statement pointing out that these characters are all Sicilians, not Italians. Also that Castro is not Italian. Fallachi is not really Italian either. True, he was born Italian but I'll bet he dosen't go to church or belong to any Italian organizations or vote Italian or anything. . . ."

"I'm against any public action," said Carrizoni. "It will only call attention to the Italian nature of the Mafia."

"What Mafia?" snorted Signato, "there *is* no Mafia! It's a myth!"

"Hold on, now," broke in Mr. Delmonica. "I agree with Carrizoni. Let's not further aggravate a bad situation. Let's accentuate the positive. Let's buy a half hour on prime time television honoring Nino Benvenuti, the former middleweight champion, and get Perry Como to m.c. and have Phil Rizzuto, Joe Pepitone, Joe DiMaggio, Judge Sirica and Gina Lollobrigida as guests, and have Correlli of the Met sing some Puccini and play up the positive Italian role in American life, like Don Ameche inventing the telephone. I bet Roma Wine or Ronzoni Spaghetti would sponsor."

"No Pepitone," muttered Signato. "Damn hippie, no field, no hit."

"Say," suggested Muzzola, "maybe we should have a private conference with the wire services and the networks and so on, and point out to them the damage from playing up this Italian angle. Why call it Cosa Nostra all the time? Why not just 'One Man's Family?' And why not give the Irish a little more attention? And you know Meyer Lansky is not exactly a paisano! And what about that gang of WASPs in the Watergate shtick? Can't we tell the public about the Kosher Nostra? Maybe we should set up a research committee to find out which of these guys are not Italians— and a publicity committee to give *them* better billing . . ."

"You folks are getting too panicky," said Mr. Autellio. "My organization, the Italian Anti-Defamation League, has been talking to people in the White House and things aren't as bad as you think. There's a good chance the President will visit Italy in his Three I tour (Italy, Ireland and Israel)—probably a few weeks before the next election—and that will wash out the memory of the Mafia."

"I still think you're all running scared," said Delmonica. "Whatever temporary harm comes from the Mafia has been canceled out by the Vatican Council and Pope Paul." He paused pensively. "People *do* remember that Paul is Italian, don't they? Could we ask the press to refer to him as Pope Paul, parenthesis, former Cardinal Montini, close parenthesis?"

Carrizoni smashed his first on the table. "Stop it! Where's your self-respect? Did the Jewish people kvetch like this every time one of their own turned up in the New York *Times* as a gonif? No! They were too busy fighting 'Bernie Loves Bridget.' Did the blacks run scared after the Panthers hit the fan? Are our backbones carved out of lasagna? Are we going to stand like men or turn chicken cacciatore? I say we have to declare war on all Italian stereotypes. Down with all these rotten Italian jokes! By the way, did you hear the one about the Italian submarine. . . . I'm sorry. I lost my head. And let's accentuate the *positive*. Tell colored and Jewish jokes. Point out all the troubles in Greece, Israel and Uganda. How many of the Watergaters were Italian? If the Jews can become an IN thing in American culture, why not Italians? If Agnew can become a household word, why not Alioto? Let's commission Philip Roth to write a book on "How to Be an Italian Mama." Let's have a play about Christopher Columbus; if we don't exploit him, the Jews or the Spaniards will claim him."

At this point, the man called Autellio (who was really Milton Goldsfine, an agent of the B'nai B'rith Anti-Defamation League, who had infiltrated the Italian

ADL) slipped out to telephone *his* ADL and, being a double agent, the FBI.

"Talk, talk, talk!" shouted Carrizoni. "Let's take to the streets. We've got to confront the Establishment, raise up the issues, Italian is beautiful!!"

"Okay, but how will we get our people to show up?" demanded Signato.

"How!?" screamed Tony. "I'll tell you how! Sure, there's no such thing as a Mafia, we all know that, but if the FBI can use the myth, so can we. So pass the word among the paisanos that the so-called Mafia *expects* them to close their shops and be on the streets for the rally!"

And so the anti-FBI rally was a huge success, attracting hundreds of thousands of protesters and dozens of politicians (except for Senator John Marchi, who sniffed at the whole thing like it was rancid fettucine) denouncing the myth of the Mafia and shouting operatic "arrivedercis" to the FBI which, of course, participated in the demonstration skillfully disguised in the person of an Italian organ grinder with (still another) monkey on his back.

XI

I'm Middle-aged—Fly Yourself

Travel would also keep you out of a rut, would broaden your interests and light your flame. But, unfortunately, YOU can't travel because you must stay near your shrink and because nobody will take care of the dog. This really seems to be the story of your life. So sit home and feel sorry for yourself, advertise for a dog-sitter and read the travel section while every other middle-aged dingaling tootles all over the globe.

Actually there are advantages to the long delays in getting your travel plans off the ground. This way you can visit all the travel agents, compare prices, collect all the folders, chart the itinerary—and then *stay home,* saving all that loot which is devaluing down the drain. So why bother with packing, passports, customs, airsickness, money conversion, traveler's checks, Michelin guides and the whole shmeer? By staying home and *preparing* for your great trip, you can build up a big head of steam of excitement and anticipation without the wear and tear of actually *traveling* and without second-mortgaging yourself to your travel agent for the next ten years (for, as your shrink reminds you: *"I'm number one"*). And, mercifully, you won't have to inflict *pictures* on helpless relatives and friends.

Remember, you are now middle-aged. You cannot travel like your son, the carpenter (whom you describe as being "in construction"), or like your daughter, the candlemaker (whom you describe as "in home furnishings"), both of whom work just long enough to pay for a round-trip youth fare to Rome, throw their jeans into a scruffy dufflebag and disappear into the wild blue yonder for months at a clip. Being youth people, they do not need reservations, maps, plans, itineraries or goals. They can hustle to the hostels. They can be impulsive and spontaneous as the spirit moves them. All they need is a little bread, their youth card and plenty of time to follow their hearts—and whims—to all the wondrous places of the world. If it were *you*, you would in advance check out friends and relatives in that part of the world, weather reports, hotel reservations and the like. But the kids belong to a strange, lovable and world-wide tribe of YOUTH PEOPLE which transcends geography, race, politics, economics and sex. They look after each other in remote beaches on Crete, in the snowy mountains of the Himalayas, on the grassy paths of Serengeti and in the desert sands of the Sinai.

You, on the other hand, would probably be mugged by a Bedouin in the Sinai or stoned at an anti-American riot in Paris. So the hell with it. Stay home and *prepare*. Travel is like sex. Anticipation is 70 per cent of the joy.

The following are the central elements in the Vorspan Stay-At-Home-and-Save-Your-Loot-Travel-Plan:

1. LEARN THE FOREIGN LANGUAGE. The one thing to

be avoided at all costs (aside from traveling itself) is to become another frenzied, automated, camera-swinging American *tourist,* "doing" a country a day in somebody's package deal. What good is France if you can't talk to Frenchmen? What good is Rome if you have to order from the American tourist menu? What good is an African safari if you cannot say "jambo" in Swahili to the waiter, or "santi sana" to the Masai tribesman on the side of the road? Without language, you are an encapsulated cultural barbarian imagining that the whole world is America.

No, if you ever really *do* travel, you must have the ability to become part of the environment of the land you visit. And that doesn't mean feverishly studying a phrase book as the plane comes in for a landing. It means setting aside several months of intensive discipline *at home,* mastering the rudiments of the language before you even allow yourself to roam into the mine field of the neighborhood travel agent. Whatever country you fancy, the native language of that country can be studied *at home* and, more than likely, in a course at the university, the Berlitz school or with a private tutor. Let us say that you have it in your head to take a trip to Israel. Why? Why not? Well, how?

Most visitors see Israel on a frantic, two-week tour, much of which is spent whizzing about with one's fellow Americans on a tour bus, dozing in catatonic exhaustion while ancient ruins race by. The tour hurtles you from the Hilton Tel Aviv, to the King David Hotel, to the Dan Carmel in Haifa, to the Galilee, to the Dead Sea and Elat, while the guide drones on about military monuments and you and your fellow tourists sink into enervated stupors. Traveling thus, you may never see the inside of a city bus, chat with an Israeli

soldier, catch a movie, meet an Arab felafel vendor or
rap with local children in a Jerusalem park. It is like
living your life in an air-conditioned bus with the
windows closed. It is an artificial extension of your
own America, transported to the Middle East. To live
like a *real person,* to become part of the life of the
people, to forswear the ways of the tourist—this is
the way to GO and to GROW. But it requires a grasp
of the *language.* Otherwise, you remain a *mere tourist,*
with that funny kibbutz cap on your head and the
omnipresent camera over your shoulder, dutifully filing
into the art gallery in Safed, into which the guide
shoves you (for twenty-seven minutes) because he
gets a rake-off from the manager. No tourist you.

So hie yourself to the nearest ulpan in your American city. An ulpan is simply an accelerated class for
learning the Hebrew language. And why shouldn't you
be able to learn the language? Why not indeed? So
you enroll either in an intensive course—six days a
week, four hours a day, for four months—or, knowing
you, in a lesser course—perhaps three days a week,
four hours a day, for three months.

Going into an ulpan is like going into analysis. It
is good for the soul, excellent salon conversation, but
it doesn't work. As with analysis, the thing to do when
you finish is to start again because it can become a
way of life. No matter. You'll still talk pidgin Hebrew.
Why? Firstly, the language is impossible. It is a language in which "who" means "he," "he" means "she"
and "me" means "who." "Dog" means "fish" and you
go from right to left. Hours are feminine, but minutes
are masculine. Ulpan Hebrew is a very special kind of
Hebrew, having no resemblance to the language Israelis
really speak. It is a kind of mandarin Hebrew, like

learning Shakespeare English. In the ulpan, one mem-
orizes charming little conversations for use in the bus,
restaurant, barbershop, store, laundry, theater, etc.
Each little scenario is pounded into your head. You
burnish it in your mind, polish it, perfect it, until the
Great Day comes when you get to Israel and go forth
to the street to try it out on the local storekeeper,
like Jane looking for Tarzan.

"Slicha," (excuse me) you say, girding yourself to
launch your hard-won conversation for use in the
store. "Ani rotzeh . . . (I want)"

"English! Talk English!" he orders. "I want to fix
my English."

(Your store conversation collapses like a house of
cards.)

It takes courage to persist when you want to practice your Hebrew on them, but they want to practice
their English on you. Moreover, one little twist of the
tongue can be a disaster. A dear friend of mine, showing off the embryonic ulpan Hebrew he had learned
in Cleveland, ordered coffee at a Haifa cafe and, beaming proudly, added "blee kelev." It was a small mis-
take. "Cholov" is cream; "kelev" is dog. He had ordered
coffee without dog. Similarly, speakers of ulpanese have
been known to ask such questions as:

"Do you have a bathroom in your arm?"

"May I buy your sister?"

"Can I sprinkle a king on your meat?"

"Is there a restaurant in the tree?"

Learning Hebrew is partly a function of your poly-
syllabic skills, if any, the grooves in your brain and
your age. Older people are not so groovy; their children
catch the language as if it were a common cold. The
result is a peculiar role reversal. When we children

of immigrants were young, our parents used to speak
in their ancient tongues when they didn't want us
to understand. In Israel, the children of American
olim (immigrants) chatter away in comfortable Hebrew while their greenhorn parents glare unhappily at
the smart alecs. It is the *kids* who use a strange language (Hebrew) to talk about their parents in their
presence, while the parents cling to the language of
the "Old Country."

One American woman listened glumly to her kids
complaining about her in machine-gun Hebrew—and
she rushed to the dictionary to find that the recurrent
word was "witch!" A famous professor of Romance
languages, master of ten languages, including Hebrew,
was wiped out in Jerusalem when his three-year-old
grandson corrected his grammar. All these frustrations
are sublimated very effectively in Israel. Women beat
their rugs on their balconies as if they had captured
Hitler singlehanded, and the men drive their cars like
Japanese kamikazes. Everyone feels better and agrees
"t'yeh tov"—it will be okay!

Thousands of western immigrants to Israel are
breaking their teeth on Hebrew years and years after
their arrival. "Hey, I've made it. In America I was
always regarded as a Jew. Here I'm regarded as an
Anglo-Saxon!" Some finally give up and content themselves with talking their native tongue to fellow immigrants. Others keep trying. One immigrant, after fifteen years of studying in ulpanim, apologized: "I only
speak in the present tense, masculine; go shoot me!"

Every day in the ulpan you play a form of "show
and tell." The teacher asks you to describe what you
did yesterday. ("I woke up. I ate breakfast. I walked
on the street.") Then, the class learns a "sicha" (con-

versation) about going to a restaurant, a post office,
a kitchen. (Some students are excellent in the barbershop and restaurant and lousy in the bedroom.)

One American completed his ulpan course in New
York City, preparatory to his "trip" to Israel. The
teacher gave him a final conversation.

"Ata m'daber Ivrit achshav?" (Do you speak Hebrew
now?)

"Oui," he replied.

"But that's French."

"Oh," he exulted, "I learned *French, too?*"

2. PLAN TO VISIT A COUNTRY OF ANTIQUITY. Listen,
you are becoming more and more preoccupied with
your advancing age. You are beginning to feel as
antique as a teapot from the Momoyama period of
Japan. Therefore, you should use travel to put your own
life into better perspective. Plan to visit one of the
fascinating lands whose origins go back to the dawn
of human history. What do you need with the shiny
newness of Brazilia? And what good will modern
Phoenix and Tucson do your aching spirit? What you
need is to stride the plains and hills whence arose
ancient man from out the glacial slime and forged the
primitive implements of civilization, the magical places
where biblical men and women pitched their tents.
How can you feel old when you stand on the edge of
Olduvai Gorge in Kenya and watch the archeologists,
scraping gently with dentist scalpels, uncovering the
remains of prehistoric man who lived in this place
five hundred thousand years ago? America seems a
newborn land, and you are a babe in the woods.

So plan to go to Africa or Egypt or China or Israel.
And plan to join a dig. It will loosen your muscles
and your imagination, and it will make you realize

that, while you may be getting on, you are not the Peking or Piltdown man. You are just a link, albeit weak, in a long human chain that stretches thousands of generations back into the murk of antiquity. Perhaps, it is true, that you are no longer at your best. But, then, let's face it, you never *were!* Nobody ever mistook you for St. Francis of Assisi!

3. PLAN A TRIP WHICH WILL RESULT IN NEW INTERESTS AND NEW HORIZONS. One of the ideal trips to *plan* is a no-shooting safari to East Africa. It is one of the mind-blowing experiences of the world, and it will shape new interests to enliven the life of your mind upon your return. The animal world truly stretches your mind and sharpens your sensitivity and imagination. You spend day after day in vast, unprotected game preserves and national parks. Each night you sleep in a lodge set down in the very midst of the wild game, usually perched on a breath-taking mountain or canyon wall. There is never a fence or barrier, because it is *their* habitat, *their* home and *you* are the visitor. You stand, for example, on the deck of Treetops, a lodge set forty feet high in a giant tree in the middle of the Aberdare National Park, and you watch the procession of *free* animals—giraffes, elephants, rhinos, impalas, gazelles—and suddenly you realize that *you* are the caged animal now; *they* are free to watch *your* human zoo. Your mind tumbles. You've always vaguely understood that human beings are not the only living creatures with rights to life and dignity. But here nature takes on new dimensions; so does life. You've grown *up* as well as older, thanks to Africa, and you may now become an animal buff, an ecology nut, a lover of zebra steak, an Africa freak and—hopefully—less of a human chauvinist.

4. ORGANIZING A TRIP (WITHOUT GOING) KEEPS YOUR
LIFE AHEAD OF YOU. This is just plain common sense.
As you break the sound barrier into middle age, you
begin to think of a fantastic trip to some exotic land
or perhaps even a trip around the world. But, once it
is done, what do you do for an encore? You have
seen the world—and it is *yours*—but you are also busted,
and what do you have to show for it except a diary
and a mountain of pictures? For the middle-ager, this
is a dangerous business. You begin to relive your trip
and, pretty soon, you are locked into the nostalgic
past. To your friends and relatives, you become a
bore ("I won't come in unless you turn off that damn
movie machine") and your present becomes an anti-
climax to the glories of your past adventure.

No, it is better to keep your trip always *ahead* of
you. It keeps the emotional juices running; it greens
your imagination. Postpone your trip along with me;
the best is yet to be. Anybody can rush off to Mexico,
Brazil or Australia and *spend* three weeks (and a
small fortune) on a lovely vacation. The trick is to
use your *projected* trip to enrich your *present* life.
And the only way to do that is to stay home, defer
pleasure, plan, dream, learn the language, become
a mavin on the culture and literature of the land and
prepare yourself with all the care which the astronauts
pour into their preparations for space. If they didn't
blast off, would they not still be astronauts?

And one thing more. There is nothing like traveling
the world to make you appreciate home, sweet home.
If in doubt, visit the chaos of Kennedy Airport on a
hot summer night as the groups go out. And, contrari-
wise, there is nothing like staying *home* to make you

appreciate the world beyond (which, of course, looks more like America every day anyway).

Therefore, in summary, it must be obvious by now that world travel can be a great trip for the middle-ager, but only if you don't actually *do* it. Doing it can be a bummer. Looking *forward* to it can be a spiritual high. I mean, what does Henry Kissinger now have to look forward to?

XII

The Male Menopause That Refreshes: Interview with an Expert, Dr. Jerry Atrick

To help us gain a greater understanding of the sociology and psychology of middle age, we interviewed Dr. Jerry Atrick, professor of sociology at Overhill College. Dr. Atrick is author of *Shoemakers' Children Go Barefoot* and several other specialized studies in professional journals. He is an expert (which is somebody who knows everything but nothing else).

Q: Dr. Atrick, what do you think is the chief problem of growing older in our society?

A: The chief problem is that syndrome compounded of a convergence of anomie, ennui, isolation and obsolescence which inheres in the cultural ambiguities of a youth-obsessed society in which nothing old is good unless it is bottled, if you get my meaning.

Q: Well, I guess so. But I'm not sure. Are you saying that older people are not valued in our society as they are in others?

A: Almost. You see, the ancient Hebrews valued the wisdom of the elderly and thus Abraham lived to be 175, Jacob 147, Joseph only 110, and Golda also well into the paint cards. The Greeks, on the other hand, went in for infanticide. What do we do? We go in for agicide, which is a term I coined to denote the practice endemic in American culture, of derogating age and segregating the oldsters into institutions like condominiums, senior citizen homes and the United States Supreme Court.

Q: Is that a reflection of the erosion of the American family?

A: What erosion? The family system is today subjected to a simultaneity of pressures of such magnitude as to render its viability of doubtful dubeity.

Q: Does that mean the American family is . . . ?

A: Kaput, finis or, as we say in Latin, ein drerd arein.

Q: That's a pretty serious charge, Dr. Atrick. Is there no way of breathing new life into the institution? If not, what new forms will take its place?

A: Let me explain you. First we had the extended family, right? Then it degenerated into the nuclear family which, of course, exploded . . . which should not be surprising to any student of nuclear physics. It goes back to Einstein's theory of relativity—too many relatives and boom, the shit hits the fan! And so now we have the atomized family, each person valuing his own individuality, doing his own thing, casting off the family unit in search of money or prestige or fame or what have you.

Q: Are families more separated today than ever before?

A: Propinquity-wise, yes. Take a typical family. The parents are divorced. He lives in Washington, waiting for the Democrats to get back in. The Ms. lives in Seattle on a houseboat where she works full time for women's lib, interrupting her work from time to time to nudge the judge to hustle up her alimony checks. They have a paradigmatic 2.6 children family. Jake, the oldest, is a transvestite in a changing neighborhood in Evanston, Illinois; Donna, the girl, is an astrologist in Palm Beach. The third child, who is only 6/10 there, lives an incomplete life in a half-cocked commune in Santa Fe. What does such a family have in common? What strands connect them?

Q: Damned if I know. Nothing, I would say.

A: Wrong. It is *love.* They *love* each other only because of the distance between them. Distance has reordered the reality of their relationships. Distance, plus nostalgia, has created a structure of ambience in which even the husband and wife, who objectively hate each other, are able to communicate with each other in love which makes the world go round.

Q: But they don't even see each other, do they?

A: Precisely.

Q: And if they did?

A: Genocide without question. This relationship can survive anything but contact. Beware of cheaper airplane rates or some other similar calamity.

Q: Let's try a different tack, Dr. Atrick.

A: Please.

Q: What do you think of second marriages?

A: Not until you get rid of the first, and I'm not crazy about the idea of the first either.

Q: Well, do you think middle age can be as much fun as youth?

A: Middle age is even funnier, as you can perceive all about you. Middle age is the fifty-yard line. When you get there, you should either kick or pass. The important thing is that you must get points on the board before you go to the eternal locker room. "When the going gets tough, the tough get going."

Q: I see. What about government? Do you think the government is doing all it can to enhance the quality of lives for middle-aged people?

A: Hell, no. We should be drafted and made to fight the wars. What do those young whippersnappers know about fighting? Most of them were never even married! No wonder Vietnam gave war a bad name!

Q: You have been doing research in the psycho-mascular ambience of middle age. What have you come up with?

A: Evidences of cranial tempestuousness and cerebral disturbance.

Q: What does that mean?

A: Middle age is a big headache.

Q: How can a man or woman age gracefully?

A: Christian Science is the ticket. Stay away from those crummy medics. It's all in the head. A friend of mine, a Christian Scientist, taught me that. His doctor told him he was dying of obesity. He laughed and told the doctor: "It's all in the head. You think I'm a *fat-head?* It's all in one's thinking." And he ignored the doctor's advice.

Q: And how is he now?

A: He *thinks* he's been dead for a year.

Q: Dr. Atrick, with the life span rising—

A: It's not rising. It's only temporary. It's just a flash in the span.

Q: But, if things are so bleak, do you see any grounds for hope?

A: Oh, indubitably. Within a generation I think all old people will be bused to condominiums in Florida, California and Arizona.

Q: Why is that good?

A: Because we will be out of danger when the President begins bombing our northern cities.

Q: Bombing our cities??!!!

A: Of course. The mayors and governors are demanding a bigger share of the federal budget which the President has impounded. In order to bring domestic peace and to permit good-faith negotiations on the basis of strength, the President will have to bomb the cities. It's a case of caveat emptor, which is Pentagonese for "Whoops, there goes New York City!"

Q: But where does that leave the older people?

A: Let's get one thing straight. The way this country is going, everyone will be old in just a few years. We are undergoing the first national experiment in pressurized aging, like two hundred million cheeses.

Q: Dr. Atrick, do you ever wish you had been born in some other era?

A: Oh, I was. In Bible times I was Onan, the Alexander Portnoy of Judea. Then I came back again in Roman times as a towel boy in the Diocletian baths. Still later, I was a deflowered virgin in Elizabethan England. Later I lost my head in Revolutionary France, my farm in Bolshevik Russia and my wallet in Central Park. I was a deep-throated prostitute on the American frontier at the turn of the century.

Q: We all know about female menopause, but is

there really a male climacteric as well? Or is it just the familiar middle-age blahs?

A: The female goes into menopause, typically, with a sharp falling off of estrogen (female sex hormones). Some experts believe there is a male menopause, resulting from the gradual decline of testosterone production. To test this thesis, I experimented with twenty relatively horny males into each of whom we pumped a full tank of testosterone (lead free) hormones while exposing them to a private screening of *Deep Throat*. Our conclusion: The fault, dear middle-aging males, is not in your testes, but in your *heads*. Women's lib is a fine movement and all of that, but, as the life of Roger Shmedbeck shows, we do *not* have to have a menopause just because *they* do!

Q: Shmedbeck? Who was Shmedbeck?

A: Shmedbeck was a sixteenth-century monk who became the first clergyman in history to leave his tongue to science. . . .

Q: But, Dr. Atrick, you are a middle-aged man. How did you escape this depression syndrome?

A: Who escaped? I've been depressed for decades. I've been mainlining testosterone for years. I don't know what I'm doing in this cockamamey work. It wasn't until 1940 that this profession began to do more good than harm. My parents are dead. My friends are sprouting coronaries. My doctor tells me I have the first signs of arteriosclerosis. My crazy kids are taller than I am, and they think I'm a shmuck. My wife bores me to tears, and I'd have an affair if I didn't have to telephone in the morning and send poems. And I wonder what the whole thing is all about! Sometimes I want to cry. What am I going to DO? *What will I be when I grow up?*

Q: Hang in there, Doctor. Tell me, Doctor, there must be millions of Americans of both sexes who feel the way you do. What advice do you give *them?*

A: There are two ways to go. One is flight. You can just withdraw into yourself, give in to your feelings of hopelessness, stop trying to get ahead. The other is fight. You can fight your fear of death and of age, work to make things better. Flight means giving up. Fight means mushing on, continuing to learn and to grow. The choice is up to each of us. We only go around once. Remember the turtle; it makes progress only when it sticks out its neck.

Q: Isn't it tough to keep fighting?

A: Yes, until you consider the alternative. I'll give you an example. Professor Rogers found that economic prosperity can contribute to marital trouble as readily as can economic hardship. He tells the story of a couple who fought their way up from poverty, succeeding handsomely in both of their professions, paying off the mortgage, calling their brokers to put money into mutual funds, becoming machers in their community. At that point, their marriage went kaput. Why? Because they were much happier when they had to fight. Psychologically, their aggressive and destructive tendencies were sublimated in coping together with outside problems. Once they coped with those, they couldn't cope with themselves and each other, and the whole marriage came a cropper.

Q: Gee, that's very interesting, Dr. Atrick. What's the ultimate solution then?

A: Change the culture. We live in a culture where the highest compliment a young person can pay an aging one is "Oh, you look so *young!*" Bullshit, my friend! If the culture venerated age, invested age with honor and dignity and a guaranteed annual income, it would be a different ball game. The high rate of suicide among oldsters comes from social isolation, loss of human esteem, inactivity, poverty, rejection. The society RESENTS the aging! Nobody will admit it, but the society believes in euthanasia!

Q: How do *you* feel about euthanasia?

A: They fight too goddam much, but the Europeans aren't much better.

Q: How can we change the culture?

A: REVOLUTION! We are the true revolutionaries; we have the time and we have nothing to lose. We should tear up the society by the short hairs. We alta cockers should discover our common oppression, zing the acne generation and fight for self-respect and our right to a piece of the action in the larger community.

Q: Please don't get so excited, Dr. Atrick. You're jumping up and down and you're turning blue.

A: I raise up angry, pal!

Q: I know, Doctor, but I don't want you to have a heart attack before we complete the interview.

A: I raise up angry because I want our generation not to rust away on our laurels, but to move mountains, to give the generations yet unborn an illustration of dignity in the face of years and of death itself!

Q: You're pulling my hair, Doctor, please calm down. Do other societies treat their old-timers any better than we do?

A: Take the Australian aborigines, my friend. When the aboriginal men get old, they are regarded as the founts of ceremonial wisdom and so they are given most of the young women, and there is not a particle of evidence that *that* depresses them one damn bit.

Q: Would that make *us* happy?

A: Don't knock it till you've tried it, son! And take the Navajo Indians. When the Navajo hits forty-five he doesn't become unemployable; he becomes a leader. He doesn't have to ride horses bare-assed any more or climb mountains or look beautiful. He is the center of the tribe, and all he has to do is give orders. And there is no evidence that he gets one of those male menopauses to which we are heir.

Q: And how long does he live?

A: To about forty-six, I think.

Q: Do you have any closing words of advice to our aging population, people fighting the ordeal of middle age?

A: My advice is don't listen to all the dreck about hormones, menopause, testosterone, glands and the whole medical shtik. If we're in trouble—and we are—it's all in our heads. So, my advice is get your head on straight!

Q: But HOW? Through individual therapy?

A: Hell, no! Man on man, nobody can cover a shrink! He'll outhustle you every time. He'll charge his own mother thirty dollars an hour to have dinner at her house!

Q: How do you feel about T-groups, then?

A: Biggest rip-off since Cain and Abel, all that touchy-feely crap!

Q: But, Dr. Atrick, if neither a shrink nor a group can cut the mustard, how *can* we get our heads on straight? Can each of us hack it alone?

A: PRAY!

Q: Pray!? Wow, I didn't know you were *religious*. I thought you were a man of science.

A: It's knowing all these brilliant idiots, stuffed with

facts but with souls parched as the Dead Sea, that turned me to religion and prayer.

Q: What do you pray for?

A: A heart of flesh instead of stone. The capacity to feel again, to love, to grow, to celebrate the only life we've got, to have the faith to shape a better and more gentle world for those who will come after us, to leave a sweet ripple in the lake of eternity.

Q: Will God hear your prayers? Will He answer?

A: She'll hear, She'll hear, but don't nudge too much. She's getting older, too, and sometimes Her children's racket drives Her up the wall and She raises up angry!